C Collins

ZODIAC
HEAVEN OR HELL

A GUIDE TO STAR SIGNS,
RELATIONSHIPS & COMPATIBILITY

SCOTLAND*on*SUNDAY

HarperCollins Publishers
Westerhill Road, Bishopbriggs, Glasgow G64 2QT

A Diagram book first created by
Diagram Visual Information Limited of
195 Kentish Town Road, London NW5 2JU

First published 1993
Last edition published 2000
This edition published for Scotsman publications 2006

ISBN 0-00-778970-X

Printed in Great Britain by Bookmarque Ltd, Croydon, Surrey

Contents

Introduction

Collins Gem Zodiac Types is a clear and concise introduction to the signs of
the zodiac and the behavioural characteristics they are believed to endow.
Each sign and its attributes have been detailed within separate chapters.
Many different aspects – from a Scorpio's personality and reactions to
situations in the workplace and at home, to a Taurean's behaviour when
in love – are described with the help of lists, panels and illustrations.

What is a sign of the zodiac?

Each of the 12 signs of the zodiac is a name given to a 30 degree arc of
the sky, as viewed from Earth. As the Earth moves round the Sun, the Sun
appears to pass from one 30 degree arc to the next, completing the
journey through all 12 zodiac arcs in one year. For example, a person
whose birthday is on 1 January is born when the Sun is in the zodiac sign
of Capricorn. This is referred to as a person's sun sign. Hence, a person
born a month later, when the sun is passing through the next 30 degree
arc, would have the next zodiac sign, Aquarius, as his sun sign.

Characteristics of the zodiac signs

The popular view is that a person will display the characteristics
associated with his or her sun sign. For example, characteristics typical of
Capricorn include ambition, faithfulness, weak knee joints and a long
lifespan. In reality, however, many people born with the Sun in Capricorn
may well have little ambition, be unfaithful, have perfect knees or may
have died young.

What is astrology?

Astrology is the study of apparent coincidences between certain events on
Earth and the positions of the Sun, Moon and eight planets. In traditional
terms, the Sun, Moon and planets (often loosely called 'the stars') are said
to influence events on Earth. The modern view, first suggested by the
psychologist Carl Gustav Jung, is that events coincide with a particular
pattern of the stars. This phenomenon is known as synchronicity.

The personal birth chart

When studying synchronicity between personality and the stars, a
complete horoscope or birth chart must be made. This shows the positions
of the Sun, Moon and planets at the time of birth, relative to the place of
birth. The birthchart indicates many features, only one of which is the
position of the sun at birth.

A sample birth chart

The symbols on the chart are the standard ones used to indicate the zodiac signs, the Sun, Moon and planets. The chart below is for a person born on 25 May 1931, therefore the Sun is in the zodiac sign of Gemini. The position of the Moon at birth, the positions of all the eight planets of the solar system and several other important features, such as geographical location, are all taken into account when interpreting the chart. For example, in the sample chart, the Moon is in Virgo, i.e. the moon sign is Virgo. The Moon is linked with mood and emotion, so astrologically this person's moods would be Virgoan, rather than Geminian. A person who had been born on the same day, in a different year and location, however, would have a chart that was differently oriented, although it would have several similar features.

In very broad, general terms, this is the basis of personal astrology.

A birth chart

See 'Astrological Symbols', p.9, for the meanings of the symbols shown

Finding your sun sign

The approximate dates of when the Sun moves into each sign are listed below. They will be correct for most years, but incorrect for others. For example, if your birthday is 22 July, some lists will say your sun sign is Cancer, as shown below, others will say Leo.

Sign	Dates
Aries	21 March – 19 April
Taurus	20 April – 20 May
Gemini	21 May – 20 June
Cancer	21 June – 22 July
Leo	23 July – 22 August
Virgo	23 August – 22 September
Libra	23 September – 22 October
Scorpio	23 October – 21 November
Sagittarius	22 November – 21 December
Capricorn	22 December – 19 January
Aquarius	20 January – 18 Febuary
Pisces	19 February – 20 March

The cusp

The exact time when the Sun moves from one sign to the next is known as the cusp or beginning of the sign. Because the movement of the earth around the sun is not exactly regular each year, the precise date when the sun moves from one sign to the next sometimes differs.

Predictions

Future events cannot be predicted. Professional astrologers read trends by comparing a person's birth chart with the day-to-day movements of the Moon and the small planets (Mercury, Venus, Mars), and the longer term movements of the larger planets (Jupiter, Saturn, Neptune, Uranus, Pluto).

Astrology and free will

In general, astrological interpretations are descriptions of how a person may behave rather than what he or she might actually do. Every characteristic has its positive and negative sides, the interpretation of which is a matter for personal choice; for example, one Taurean characteristic is never to change without very good reason. This could be interpreted either as undying loyalty or as stubborn resistance.

How to enjoy this book

The information about each zodiac sign is a summary of the main characteristics associated with it. If you find that you happen to be typical of your sun sign, it is probably because several planets are in your sign or are linked with it in positive ways. If you have few or none of its characteristics, it could be that:

1 other signs are stronger in your chart;

2 your full potential has not yet emerged;

3 the characteristic has negative 'influences' in the orientation of your chart, which you have controlled;

4 your birth date is the day of a cusp and the exact time of birth may indicate that your sun sign is actually in the next, or previous, sign.

Reading the sun signs is fun, and may be revealing. If, however, you wish to investigate astrology further, the best course of action is to have a full chart made and interpreted by a qualified astrologer.

Astrological symbols

The symbols used to represent the signs and their ruling planets are depicted below.

Sign	Symbol	Ruling planets	Symbols
Aries	♈	Mars	♂
Taurus	♉	Venus	♀
Gemini	♊	Mercury	☿
Cancer	♋	Moon	☽
Leo	♌	Sun	☉
Virgo	♍	Mercury	☿
Libra	♎	Venus	♀
Scorpio	♏	Mars	♂♇
Sagittarius	♐	Jupiter	♃
Capricorn	♑	Saturn	♄
Aquarius	♒	Saturn	♄♅
Pisces	♓	Jupiter	♃♆

Aries: the Ram

21 March – 19 April

The first sign of the zodiac is concerned with ● self-assertion, initiation, new beginnings ● action, daring, challenge, adventure ● exploration, pioneering, discovering ● aggression, creativity, personal goals ● personal control of everything ● competition, winning, being first ● courage, honesty, nobility, openness

Elemental quality

Aries is the cardinal fire sign of the zodiac. It can be likened to a fire which gives direction, such as in a rocket, a gun or an engine. Superman and Superwoman, who can propel themselves in any direction, are good metaphors of Aries energy. Fire is a process that causes change and Aries uses energy to bring about changes. Being a cardinal sign, Aries is the most energetic of the fire signs and usually takes the initiative.

Spiritual goal

To learn the meaning of selfless love.

THE ARIEN PERSONALITY

These are the general personality traits found in people who are typical of Aries. An unhappy or frustrated Aries may display some of the not-so-attractive traits.

Secret Aries

Inside anyone who has strong Aries influences is a person who thinks that he or she is more interesting than others and better than those with whom they are in competition. It is patently obvious to all that Aries is interested in winning, whoever or whatever the challenge. A fight, a race, a bit of physical or verbal sparring or an opportunity to do things in new ways are what keep the Aries' fires burning bright. Aries is an original, and being first lights him or her up. Aries has to be number one in every respect. The secret fear of a typical Aries is that he or she won't be liked or valued, even though a winner. However, failure is never a problem because Aries doesn't know the word ... every outcome is seen as a part of the winning process, which is why warnings of impending disasters are usually ignored.

CHARACTERISTICS	
Positive	**Negative**
• Is a leader	• Must be the boss
• Is energetic	• Brashness
• Helps others to achieve their dreams	• Blind to his or her effect on others
• Accepts challenges	• Intolerance
• Believes the best of others	• Jealousy
• Takes risks for others	• Doesn't listen
• Defends the vulnerable	• Selfishness
• An Aries life is an open book	• Impulsiveness
• Will give life for the loved one	• Poor judge of character
• Continues action even if others give up	• Dislikes being told what to do

THE ARIEN LOOK

People who exhibit the physical characteristics distinctive of the sign of Aries look tall and bold. Usually lean, they have strong bodies and may even be quite athletic. They are usually concerned to project a physical image of success. They need to be winners and generally do their very best to look the part. Appearances are important to Aries.

Physical appearance

• Body: lean and strong, with large bones, thick shoulders and a rather long neck • The face is usually long and the eyes are steady and somewhat piercing – not looking through you, but certainly looking at you, as if to challenge • There may be a scar on the face or the body from a past fight – if so it will be 'worn' with a certain pride like a winner's trophy

THE ARIES MALE

Appearance

The typical Aries man • has a strong body • is extremely energetic • has a dominating sex appeal • walks with an air of nobility • dresses in clothes appropriate to the current challenge

Behaviour and personality traits

The typical Aries man • is fiercely competitive • is honest • appears to be self-assured • takes initiative and expects others to follow • is enterprising • dreads physical disability • has very clear goals • will put his partner on a pedestal • needs to win • uses wit and brains to get what he wants

THE ARIES FEMALE

Appearance

The typical Aries woman • is slim and strong • is very active and glows with energy • has strong, luxurious hair • wears sophisticated colours and perfume • dresses in clothes appropriate to the occasion

Behaviour and personality traits

The typical Aries woman • looks you in the eye and gives a firm handshake • is enthusiastic and optimistic • talks back and often gets hurt because of it • expects loyalty • is fearless • has interests outside the home or has a career • expects to win through in any situation • is direct, open and honest • can make miracles happen

YOUNG ARIES

If a child behaves in a way that is distinctive of the personality associated with the zodiac sign of Aries, he or she will have a tendency towards the characteristics listed below.

Behaviour and personality traits

The typical Aries child • has a strong, active body and mind • has a temper when thwarted • usually walks and talks early • wants attention and to be in charge • can be lazy until someone claims to be better • is generous with toys • has a vivid, practical imagination • can achieve much in a short time • is normally very affectionate • has an inexhaustible curiosity • gets over childhood fevers very quickly

ARIES AT HOME

If a person has the personality that is typical of those born with an Aries sun sign, home is a place to come back to after many adventures, and she or he will have a tendency towards the characteristics listed below.

Typical behaviour and abilities

When at home, an Aries man or woman • wants to be the top dog • makes a substantial and secure home • doesn't like to feel tied down or restricted • will generously give money, goods and space to those who need it • can turn a hand to anything but doesn't enjoy those little jobs needed to run and repair a home

ARIES AT WORK

At work, the person who has a typical Aries personality will exhibit the following characteristics.

Typical behaviour and abilities

A typical Aries at work ● is loyal and enthusiastic about the company ● will work all hours and is not a clock-watcher ● will look elsewhere for an opening if bored ● is highly creative and can initiate ● has very strong willpower ● is not suited to political work

Aries as employer

A typical Aries boss (male or female) ● is idealistic and needs the faith of his or her employees and expects their loyalty ● believes he/she can make the future a success ● needs others but will go it alone when necessary ● wants to be recognized as the boss ● can pull a business up from near bankruptcy ● is generous with rewards for hard work ● expects everyone to drop everything to solve a crisis

Aries as employee

A typical Aries employee (male or female) ● works best when answerable only to the boss ● can promote anything ● tends to work late rather than early ● looks for opportunity to learn and progress ● intends to succeed but is careless with details ● knows he or she can do well ● will move to another job if he or she feels the challenges in the current job have run out; security is not a priority, although Aries workers usually make their way under the most difficult circumstances

Typical occupations

Aries is associated with work which inspires activity in others; for example, leaders, directors, foremen or any job that has authority. Aries must be in command or they will lose interest. Aries works best at the initiation of a project, leaving the consolidation to other people. Typical jobs are in recruitment and training, work in the theatre, business enterprises, politics, sport, and the military in any position that has power.

ARIES AND LOVE

To Aries, love is a conquest. Male Aries love the chase and seem to have little difficulty attracting women, while female Aries also love the challenge of the hunt but go about it a little more subtly. Aries of both sexes are attractive because of their natural energy. Aries in love will have many of the characteristics listed below.

Behaviour when in love

The typical Aries ● is very romantic and believes in courtly love ● will insist on doing the chasing and cannot bear to be chased by anyone ● can be extremely possessive of the lover but cannot understand if the lover is possessive ● places the loved one on a pedestal ● will be jealous of any attention the loved one gives to others ● will defend the loved one to the death

Expectations

The typical Aries expects • total faithfulness from the partner • the lover to respond as if he or she is the first and best lover ever known • to be loved exclusively • never to be criticized

The end of an affair

Boredom is the blight of most Aries love affairs. Like the knight in a crusade, it is the winning that is the peak of excitement. Once the fair lady (or fair gentleman) is won, there may be nothing left to stimulate the affair further. At this point the Aries will get itchy feet and want to be off to find new conquests. It isn't that love itself is merely a conquest, it is the joy of overcoming obstacles to reach love. The partner of an Aries must always keep a little mystery in reserve and must always believe in every new Aries dream. If all fails – and Aries will try and try before leaving a relationship – then the Aries passion cools and there remains only a lack of interest. A lover who hurts Aries very deeply can expect to be totally frozen out and ignored.

ARIES AND SEX

In many ways the excitement is in the chase not the conquest. It isn't that Aries lovers aren't faithful – they are, so long as the excitement of new challenges in love are always there to stimulate them. Aries may appear to want to dominate, but does not want a submissive partner in sex. Routine is what brings boredom to lovemaking for Aries. Aries woman may have difficulties in love because she may see her partner as a fellow contestant in the world.

ARIES AND PARTNER

The person who contemplates becoming the marriage or business partner of a typical Aries must realize that Aries will want to be in control of all the major decisions. He or she will be happy to leave the day-to-day details to a partner, but will always expect to be in overall control. Given this, the person who partners Aries can expect an exciting, creative relationship with unexpected surprises and plenty of affection.

Aries man as partner

He will want a partner of whom he can be proud, yet who will never do anything better than he can. A clever partner would be wise to be modest about personal abilities and to put effort into supporting and encouraging the sensitive Aries partner in his own dreams. In marriage, the Aries husband will regard his wife as the queen of his domain and she must behave accordingly, never failing in her loyalty to him and keeping surprises up her sleeve to stimulate his interest.

Aries woman as partner

Like her male counterpart, the Aries partner must always come first. This makes life difficult for the typical Aries wife in a male-dominant situation. She needs a husband who will recognize and accept her powers. A man must have self-respect and tact to partner an Aries woman. In return, both male and female Aries will bring bountiful energy, enthusiasm and loyalty to any partnership.

ARIES AND FRIENDS

In general Aries likes a friend who is special in some particular way and who will regard Aries as his or her best friend (never the second best!).

Positive factors

Aries friends are warm and hospitable but they are not usually interested in entertaining for its own sake; they usually have a reason for inviting friends around. Many Aries prefer to go out for a meal, to find an unusual eating place. Both male and female Aries usually get on better with male friends.

Negative factors

Because Aries are very jealous of other people's abilities and achievements, Aries friendships often don't last very long. However, a person who will admire his or her Aries friend and remain interesting him- or herself, though not ambitious, can enjoy an enduring friendship with Aries. Aries can become quite harsh and nasty if his or her fragile ego is under threat. A compatibility chart, overleaf, lists those with whom Aries is likely to have the most satisfactory relationships.

ARIEN LEISURE INTERESTS

Most typical Aries enjoy some physical activity that allows him or her to display their prowess. Aries may also enjoy board games that give them the opportunity to demonstrate their superior mental and tactical power. On the whole, typical Aries pursue the following leisure interests: ● competitive sports, e.g. football, tennis ● driving a car which has a great image ● racing by car, bicycle or on foot ● risky physical activities, such as sailing round the world single-handed or climbing a new peak ● military pastimes ● theatrical activities

COMPATIBILITY CHART

In general, if people are typical of their zodiac sign, relationships between Aries and other signs (including the complementary opposite sign, Libra) are as shown below

	Harmonious	Difficult	Turbulent
Aries	●		
Taurus	●		
Gemini	●		
Cancer		●	
Leo	●		
Virgo			●
Libra		●	
Scorpio			●
Sagittarius	●		
Capricorn		●	
Aquarius	●		
Pisces	●		

ARIEN LIKES AND DISLIKES

Likes

- being liked ● the best wines ● a unique number plate on the car
- money to use ● new clothes ● red roses ● colourful food
- personalized gifts ● presents wrapped in intriguing paper
- new books ● diamonds

Dislikes

- being ignored ● physical restriction ● being placed less than first
- feeling hungry ● anyone who performs better than them ● old things, second-hand stuff ● having to wait for anything ● lingering after food
- bland food

Taurus: the bull

20 April - 20 May

The second sign of the zodiac is concerned with ● beauty, romance, sentimentality, sensuality ● materialistic values, wealth, prosperity ● nature, harmony, love of living things ● possession, control, security, dependability ● habit, organization, tenacity, kindness ● shyness, cautiousness, trustworthiness, calmness ● appreciation of values, talents, abilities

Elemental quality

Taurus is the fixed earth sign of the zodiac. It can be likened to an ancient rainforest full of enduring trees and rare plants that is teeming with the beauty of life, or to a beautiful, old French château that is full of valuable antiques, and which has an established vineyard and garden that offer all manner of delights to the senses. This sign represents an enduring, practical reality.

Spiritual goal

To learn the value of insight.

THE TAUREAN PERSONALITY

These are the general personality traits found in people who are typical of Taurus. An unhappy or frustrated Taurus may display some of the not-so-attractive traits.

Secret Taurus

Inside anyone who has strong Taurus influences is a person who takes the long-term view and proceeds slowly but surely, because Taurus is only interested in the very best of everything. Taurus loves to luxuriate in sensual delights and desires secure material prosperity. The two secret fears of Taurus are of being disturbed or of being left wanting. Taurus will wait for anything, even to get angry. When Taureans do eventually have to express anger, it can be devastating and is so disturbing to themselves that it takes a while for them to recover both their composure and their self-esteem.

CHARACTERISTICS	
Positive	**Negative**
• A careful and conservative outlook	• A tendency to be self-indulgent
• Dependable and offers enduring loyalty	• Can be stubborn, obstinate and get stuck in a rut
• Calm and patient	• Materialistic
• Artistic	• Slow-moving
• Thorough	• Little to say
• Attentive	• Delays action by lengthy pondering
• Values the talents of others	• Easily embarrassed
• Very loving	• Boring
• Resourceful	• Insensitivity
• Gentle and placid	
• Excellent cook	
• Good sense of time and is orderly	

THE TAUREAN LOOK

People who exhibit the physical characteristics distinctive of the sign of Taurus look as if they are well rooted and in touch with the earth. They may be plump or slim, but either way they will walk with a slightly ponderous gait, as if each step has been carefully considered. All typical Taureans have a presence which emanates solid reliability.

Physical appearance

• Body compact and sturdy, often with thick, muscular legs and thighs • Face rounded with a clear, often beautiful complexion • Neck is short and may appear rather thick if the shoulders are high and square, which is typical of those with a very strong Taurean influence • Typical Taurean feet are large or broad • Eyes are usually large and offer a steady gaze

THE TAURUS MALE

Appearance

The typical Taurus man • has a stocky body, which is muscular if he does a lot of physical activity • may be plump • will bear the discomfort of an injury or disability with extreme stoicism • has very clear skin • is likely to have plenty of hair and can grow a substantial beard • walks with determination

Behaviour and personality traits

The typical Taurus man • rarely changes his point of view • works hard to build security • is astute and can evaluate a situation very quickly in financial terms • is quiet and has a low-key charm • is unpretentious • enjoys comfort

● can be defensive and suspicious in a new or unexpected situation
● is wary of others taking advantage of him ● dresses to create an image of
respectability ● uses influential connections to get what he wants

THE TAURUS FEMALE

Appearance
The typical Taurus woman ● tends to have a rounded body ● has a beautiful
complexion and hair which always looks in excellent condition ● may live by a
very strict diet to attain slimness ● has an air of mystery about her because
she does not flaunt her sexuality ● wears clothes which give her sensual
pleasure ● has a strong body capable of hard work

Behaviour and personality traits
The typical Taurus woman ● is an introvert ● has considerable moral and
emotional courage ● takes people as they come ● is very loyal to her friends
and sticks by them if they are in trouble ● has practical common sense ● is
deeply sensual ● prefers the real to the artificial, e.g. real flowers, real silk and
genuine, high-quality antiques

YOUNG TAURUS

Behaviour and personality traits
The typical Taurus child ● is usually a quiet baby with rare outbursts ● is
stubborn and wants his or her own way ● has a strong little body and can
often be found clenching his or her fists when opposed ● is usually calm,
pleasant and a little shy ● is cuddly and affectionate ● dislikes being the
centre of attention ● responds to common sense and affection ● usually
works slowly but steadily at school

TAURUS AT HOME

If a person has the personality that is typical of those born with a Taurus sun
sign, home is a place to feel absolutely secure and comfortable. The person
who has strong Taurean influences will have a tendency towards the
characteristics listed below.

Typical behaviour and abilities
When at home, a Taurus man or woman ● hates anything to be moved around
● enjoys comfort and luxury ● has well-tried habits and likes a well-ordered
household ● prefers to own his or her home ● makes his or her home a castle
and usually fills it with furniture that will increase in value

TAURUS AT WORK

At work, the person who has a typical Taurean personality will exhibit the following characteristics.

Typical behaviour and abilities

A typical Taurus at work ● cannot bear interference ● will work towards achieving what he/she values ● has great respect for institutions ● requires work that gives respectability

Taurus as employer

A typical Taurus boss (male or female) ● patiently tests out the employees ● doggedly sticks to his stated principles ● will give everyone more than a fair chance but sack anyone who breaks his or her trust ● is often a self-made person and will make money ● does not make hasty judgements ● wants things done his or her way ● is kind and patient but expects total loyalty ● likes plain facts and hates flattery

Taurus as employee

A typical Taurus employee (male or female) ● needs a regular salary ● is an excellent person to handle money ● is honest and dependable ● is practical, sensible and down-to-earth ● enjoys sensible routines ● displays foresight ● is rarely thrown off-balance ● can handle emergencies

Typical occupations

Taurus is associated with banking, farming, floristry, interior design, architecture, food, engineering, building, general medical practice, executive secretarial positions, stable occupations in established institutions and any occupation that involves the shrewd acquisition of land, investments or goods.

TAURUS AND LOVE

To Taurus, love is a physical, sensual romance which can be expected to last for ever. Taureans are attracted by physical beauty and are very sensitive to perfume, colour, light and sound. Taurus in love will have many of the characteristics listed below.

Behaviour when in love

The typical Taurus ● is devoted and steadfast ● settles quickly into a stable affair ● loves glamour ● is extremely vulnerable to people who accept his or her affection but only want a flirtation ● will never forgive a betrayal ● the male is generally the strong silent type ● the female is usually an earth mother/Venus

Expectations

The typical Taurus expects ● his woman to be very feminine ● her man to be all male ● a promise to be kept and never broken ● a wholesome, natural

approach to physical love ● to be pampered ● to wait for a commitment
to be made

The end of an affair

It takes a long time for a Taurean to decide to leave a relationship. Taurus finds
it extremely difficult to be convinced he or she was wrong about a person.
However, once the Taurean mind is made up, there is never any turning back.
He or she will walk away for ever. Being a good judge of character is not one of
Taurus's strengths, so some will assume all is well, even when a lover is being
deceitful. When a deceit is revealed, Taurus will be very hurt but will still hang
on in hope. Some Taurus men can be rather macho, so when a relationship is
ending, the macho Taurus can lose his normally gentle approach, becoming
harsh and domineering. This usually indicates the hurt to his ego, which at
heart is very trusting and naive. The lover who walks out on a Taurean will
leave behind a bewildered, disbelieving person, who may suffer one vague
illness after another as the hurt and rage slowly come to the surface.

TAURUS AND SEX

When a typical Taurus makes love it is the most physical and natural pleasure
in the whole world. Sex is never a power game for a Taurean, it is something
very natural to be enjoyed. Taureans, especially females, are sometimes
embarrassed about their bodies if they feel they are being criticized. On the
whole, Taurus regards nudity as natural and wholesome.

TAURUS AND PARTNER

The person who contemplates becoming the marriage or business partner of a
typical Taurus must realize that Taurus will expect absolute loyalty through
thick and thin and will probably want to establish a routine way of doing things
his or her way. Given this, the person who partners Taurus can expect honest
devotion, a long-term relationship and a partner who can keep his or her head
in any emergency.

Taurus man as partner

He will want a partner who enjoys his way of doing things. The partner should
be prepared to take the responsibility for good public relations while Taurus
works quietly away ensuring that money and power come their way. The
Taurean husband wants a marriage partner whom he can possess, body, soul
and dowry. He needs a woman who enjoys physical love, since to Taureans
there is no division between love, sex and marriage.

Taurus woman as partner

She will want a partner who is attentive and appreciative. Common sense is essential in any partner of a Taurean. She, like her male counterpart, will look for a business partner who will bring prestige to the business. The Taurean wife wants to be given gifts and treated with gentleness. She does not want to be patronized, but she does want her man to remember her birthday and other anniversaries. She needs a husband who will let her organize at least a part of his life and who will never, never give her cause for jealousy.

TAURUS AND FRIENDS

In general Taurus likes a friend who is reliable, unchanging and not given to sudden excitement or changes of plans.

Positive factors

Taureans are very warm and affectionate towards their friends. They enjoy friendship with people who have good taste and with whom they can enjoy a quiet conversation or a visit to a concert or a football match. They will enjoy people who have strength of character and qualities of endurance like their own. Towards such friends, Taurus will always be gentle, kind, loving and totally trustworthy.

Negative factors

Taurus can be jealous of any attention a friend gives to someone else. Taurus does not like signs of weakness, physical or emotional, and can be quite direct about them. Taurus prizes friends who have some power which they can share and enjoy. People who wear cheap perfume, artificial fabrics and have houses that are built to deceive the eye, e.g. not real stone but stone-faced, are unlikely to attract the friendship of a typical Taurean. A compatibility chart, opposite, lists those with whom Taurus is likely to have the most satisfactory relationships.

TAUREAN LEISURE INTERESTS

On the whole, typical Taureans pursue the following leisure interests:
● collecting things of value ● singing or listening to music ● gardening
● painting ● the quieter sports ● activities that give Taurus a chance to enjoy physical pleasure, such as horse-riding

COMPATIBILITY CHART

In general, if people are typical of their zodiac sign, relationships between Taurus and other signs (including the complementary opposite sign, Scorpio) are as shown below

	Harmonious	Difficult	Turbulent
Taurus	●		
Gemini	●		
Cancer	●		
Leo		●	
Virgo	●		
Libra			●
Scorpio		●	
Sagittarius			●
Capricorn	●		
Aquarius		●	
Pisces	●		
Aries	●		

TAUREAN LIKES AND DISLIKES

Likes

- soft, sensual textures ● sensual pleasures ● a good bank balance
- certainty and well-tried routines ● gifts of value, attractively wrapped
- savouring the moments of pleasure at the table ● doing the same thing over and over

Dislikes

- being disturbed ● change ● lending things ● being told to hurry up
- sleeping in strange beds

Gemini: the Twins

21 May – 20 June

The third sign of the zodiac is concerned with ● communication, articulation, speech ● dexterity, nimbleness, light-footedness ● wit, instinct, persuasion, change, variety ● movement, curiosity, exploration, short journeys ● education, learning, collecting facts ● attention to details, adaptability ● intellect, intuition, youth, freedom

Elemental quality

Gemini is the mutable air sign of the zodiac. It can be likened to the wind in that it is constantly on the move in all its variety. Air is a metaphor for the invisible thoughts and ideas that motivate Gemini, such as the intellect, the intuition and the natural instincts. The quality known as mutable means adaptable, changeable, agreeable. Gemini constantly adjusts ideas in an attempt to create harmony.

Spiritual goal

To learn how to cooperate.

THE GEMINIAN PERSONALITY

These are the general personality traits found in people who are typical of Gemini. An unhappy or frustrated Gemini may display some of the not-so-attractive traits.

Secret Gemini

Inside anyone who has strong Gemini influences is a person who secretly longs to find his or her true soul-mate, the mysterious twin who will make the Gemini feel complete. The more self-aware Geminis will realize in maturity that the wholeness they seek is to be found within, by gathering together their many parts, especially the earthly twin with the spiritual twin. Few people listening to a confident Gemini talk would ever imagine that the inner Gemini is often feeling desperately alone and lost. Communication is a life-line to Gemini.

CHARACTERISTICS	
Positive	**Negative**
• Inquisitive	• Restless
• Entertaining and charming	• Quickly bored
• Versatile	• Impractical
• Liberal, broad minded	• Impatient and irritable
• Youthful	• Capricious and fickle
• Quick	• Gossipy
• Stimulating	• Nervous
• Inventive	• Manipulative
• Never prejudiced	• Non-committal
	• Dual personality

THE GEMINIAN LOOK

People who exhibit the physical characteristics distinctive of Gemini look tall and upright. The youthful look is typical of Gemini. People who always look younger than their actual age, at any stage of life, will have a strong Gemini influence somewhere in their birthchart. Most typical Geminians are light on their feet, regardless of their body size.

Physical appearance

• Body: usually slim. However, if the zodiac neighbours of Gemini, Taurus and Cancer, are present in the birthchart they may affect the body-build, because the signs of both Taurus and Cancer can lead to plumpness. A strong Taurus influence, particularly, can lead to a weight problem. • Generally tall • Strong and active • Long arms and legs • Fleshy hands

THE GEMINI MALE

Appearance

The typical Gemini man • is taller than average • has a pale, rough complexion that will become weather-beaten easily • is very agile • has a high forehead and receding hairline • has quick, darting eyes

Behaviour and personality traits

The typical Gemini man • is eager and always on the move • is friendly and persuasive • can sell almost anything to almost anyone • has a great deal of nervous energy • can talk himself out of difficulties • can do two things at once • likes people • is adroit, diplomatic and socially able • may change his occupation frequently • is intelligent and witty

THE GEMINI FEMALE

Appearance
The typical Gemini woman ● is tall and slender, unless there is a strong Taurus influence causing plumpness ● has very fine eyes ● has long arms and legs ● has exquisitely expressive hands ● moves quickly

Behaviour and personality traits
The typical Gemini woman ● is a lively conversationalist ● has many interests ● is a composite of many personalities ● is a great friend, taking an interest in any new subject ● will want to have a career ● seeks true romance but finds it hard to settle down ● is a deep thinker and often very intuitive ● will never turn down a cry for help ● is optimistic ● notices every detail ● can be charming and very persuasive

YOUNG GEMINI

If a child behaves in a way that is distinctive of the personality associated with the zodiac sign of Gemini, he or she will have a tendency towards the characteristics listed below.

Behaviour and personality traits
The typical Gemini child ● can seem to be in two places at once ● loves chattering ● will become irritable if cooped up ● needs lots of space to explore ● is friendly ● is bright and alert ● can be quite precocious ● usually learns to read very quickly ● likes to use his or her hands and fingers ● may be ambidextrous ● can often mimic others

GEMINI AT HOME

If a person has the personality that is typical of those born with a Gemini sun sign, home is a place to return to after yet another period of travel. The Gemini at home will have a tendency towards the characteristics listed below.

Typical behaviour and abilities
When at home, a Gemini man or woman ● likes space to move about in ● will enjoy using gadgets and all the latest technology, especially information technology ● considers a telephone absolutely essential ● will have some form of transport standing by so he or she can take off on the spur of the moment ● will have a bright, cheerful home, surrounded by the evidence of many interests ● enjoys company ● has a deep need for tenderness and emotional warmth for which he or she finds it very hard to ask

GEMINI AT WORK

At work, the person who has a typical Gemini personality will exhibit the following characteristics.

Typical behaviour and abilities

A typical Gemini at work ● gets things done ● works better with people around ● can deal with emergencies quickly ● will try anything once ● needs variety

Gemini as employer

A typical Gemini boss (male or female) ● is not dogmatic ● delegates astutely and concentrates on schemes to increase profits and cut costs ● makes changes to improve communication and productivity ● is impatient with mundane administration ● will inspect, notice and question every aspect of every department ● will classify his or her workers' talents ● enjoys building goodwill and large order books by meeting clients in restaurants, on the golf course, or anywhere out on the road in places near or far

Gemini as employee

A typical Gemini employee (male or female) ● can charm his or her way through an interview ● is good at thinking, new ideas and details ● chats, makes jokes and gets things done ● will get bored and fail to carry through an idea if too much red tape holds up a project ● enjoys fast action and quick returns

Typical occupations

Geminis are good in any kind of work that involves public relations, selling or getting information and ideas across to others such as lecturing, journalism and work in any of the media. Their quick minds, combined with dextrous abilities, make some into surgeons, scientific researchers, artists or musicians. Because they love words and ideas, they may become politicians or actors.

GEMINI AND LOVE

To Gemini, love is a romantic ideal which can only be achieved with the soul-mate. Consequently, many Geminis may flirt and have frequent affairs, looking for that perfect romantic love. The characteristics of Gemini in love are listed below.

Behaviour when in love

The typical Gemini ● is overwhelmed by confusing emotions ● may appear cool and distant ● will think things through rather than act spontaneously ● needs a rational understanding of love ● tends to repress very strong emotions ● is acutely sensitive and open to hurt ● can become emotionally dependent ● feels very deeply but finds it very hard to express love

Expectations

The typical Gemini expects ● to be understood ● the partner to be an
emotional telepath ● sympathy and tenderness ● personal freedom for self
and partner ● to enjoy flirting ● faithfulness of partner

The end of an affair

An affair will end when a Gemini gets bored or when a partner begins to make
too many emotional demands or restrict the Gemini's personal freedom. The
end may seem like a sudden decision, but it never is; the decision to leave a
lover will have been made only after much mental unhappiness. Once the
decision has been made, Geminis have no difficulty in communicating that an
affair is at an end, they just cool off, freeze the partner out or vanish. If the
partner ends the relationship, Gemini will be deeply hurt and feel insecure and
at a loss. The more outward Geminis may hide these feelings behind a sudden
outburst of scathing anger, while the quieter ones will probably try to look cool.
Either way, Gemini will put on a show of confidence and continue searching for
perfect love.

GEMINI AND SEX

When a typical Gemini makes love it is often a drive to express all their pent-
up emotions at once. Geminis seek variety in love, enjoy surprises and plenty
of light-hearted romance. Geminis are often not interested in sex for its own
sake, they want more from a partner, even in a short relationship, such as
companionship and warmth. Love and sex belong together in the eyes of a
Gemini. The most erogenous zone of a typical Gemini is the mind. Talk excites,
while silence turns off the Gemini.

GEMINI AND PARTNER

The person who contemplates becoming the marriage or business partner of a
typical Gemini must realize that Gemini has probably already had more than
one partner and will not stay long with a person who either clings or dominates.
Given this, the person who partners a Gemini can expect the talents of at least
six people wrapped up in the one Gemini.

Gemini man as partner

He will want a partner who will never attempt to dominate him, nor bore him
with endless personal problems. He will be drawn either to someone who will
help him on his way up the professional or social scale, or a person who will
stimulate him with bright ideas. Because he loves to travel, he will be delighted
in a partner who will travel with him – or accept his absences without
question.

GEMINI AND FRIENDS   29

Gemini woman as partner

She will be attracted to a person who can give her emotional security where she can relax and enjoy expressing her many talents, and her 'multi-personality'. Often the partnership will be short-lived because the restless Gemini nature always wants to be on the move. Many partners fail to understand the need of the mercurial butterfly to have a partner who will fly with her, helping her to find the peace she truly desires.

GEMINI AND FRIENDS

In general, Gemini likes a friend who is curious about the world and enjoys lively, intelligent conversation.

Positive factors

Geminis generally enjoy people who respond to, or suggest, spontaneous activities. They will run to your help when you are in need. A Gemini friend is full of life, often a Peter Pan, and always eager to be off on a new adventure. They will keep friends amused with endless stories, bits of information or network gossip.

Negative factors

Gemini never wants to miss a thing, and so may be inclined to be early or late for a meeting. Stretching or elaborating the truth is not uncommon; Geminis can hardly resist adding extra spice to make it more interesting. A compatibility chart, overleaf, lists those with whom Gemini is likely to have the most satisfactory relationships.

GEMINIAN LEISURE INTERESTS

Most typical Geminis like communication, such as conversation, radio, television, the telephone, letter writing, sending postcards and faxes. On the whole, typical Geminis pursue the following leisure interests: ● 'light' sports, e.g. table tennis, archery, darts, snooker, pool ● travel, short or long journeys ● newspapers, magazines, quizzes, crosswords ● public-speaking, variety shows, dancing ● discovering and exploring something new ● learning and using languages ● using hands and fingers for crafts, etc.

COMPATIBILITY CHART

In general, if people are typical of their zodiac sign, relationships between Gemini and other signs (including the complementary opposite sign, Sagittarius) are as shown below

	Harmonious	Difficult	Turbulent
Gemini	●		
Cancer	●		
Leo	●		
Virgo		●	
Libra	●		
Scorpio			●
Sagittarius		●	
Capricorn			●
Aquarius	●		
Pisces		●	
Aries	●		
Taurus	●		

GEMINIAN LIKES AND DISLIKES

Likes

● being free to move about ● the excitement of travel ● chatting ● telephones, gadgets, instant food ● acting as devil's advocate ● doing several things at once ● knowledge, information ● acting quickly on decisions ● variety, novelty, change ● company; being among people ● pseudonyms ● getting to the bottom of things

Dislikes

● listening to endless complaints ● regimentation ● not knowing what's going on ● wasting time ● being kept waiting ● making irrevocable commitments ● being defeated ● fixed ideas ● having to concentrate on only one thing for a long time

Cancer: the Crab

21 June - 22 July

The fourth sign of the zodiac is concerned with ● receptivity, sensitivity, defence ● home, protection, comfort, domesticity ● food, nurture, mothering instincts ● nostalgia, sentiment, roots, antiques ● money, business, response to public need ● dreams, the psychic, telepathy, etc. ● family, history, memory, patriotism

Elemental quality

Cancer is the cardinal water sign of the zodiac. It can be likened to a safe harbour where boats can take shelter from the dangers on the sea of life. Water finds its own level – it settles. The metaphorical harbour is the way Cancer provides a safe and organized place for human activity, setting each ship in its allotted place.

Spiritual goal

To learn how to take a balanced view of things.

THE CANCERIAN PERSONALITY

These are the general personality traits found in people who are typical of this sign. An unhappy or frustrated Cancerian may display some of the not-so-attractive traits.

Secret Cancer

Inside anyone who has strong Cancerian influences is a person who was very shy when young and who still tends to use a hard outer shell in defence against what are perceived as hurts from other people. The most vulnerable part of the Cancerian personality is an inner fear of nameless dangers that often reduce a wonderful dream to a pessimistic worry. This indefinable fear of insecurity is often what drives the typical Cancerian personality to invest much time and effort in activities which will enhance a feeling of security and self-preservation.

CHARACTERISTICS

Positive	Negative
• Tenacious	• Possessive
• Shrewd and intuitive	• Too easily hurt
• Kind	• Moody
• Compassionate	• Crabby
• Domesticated	• Matriarchal
• Good memory	• Holds on to insults
• Helpful	• Selfish
• Caring	• Manipulative
• Sensitive to need	• Introspective
• Protective	• Overpowering

THE CANCERIAN LOOK

People who exhibit the physical characteristics distinctive of the sign of Cancer are of three facial types. Whichever type they are, they have very expressive faces. Every mood, emotion and fleeting response shows in the changing features of the Cancerian face.

Physical appearance

• Body: usually top heavy; can be slim, but often on the plump side • Face 1: crab-like with large head, high cheekbones and prominent brows. Eyes small and far apart • Face 2: rather moon-like and baby-faced, round with soft skin, a wide mouth and a charming grin. Eyes are usually round • Face 3: a combination of the two above, but distinctive, with especially strong cheekbones

THE CANCER MALE

Appearance

The typical Cancer man • has a fairly bony structure • may have remarkable teeth, perhaps prominent, irregular or in some way unusual • if crab-faced, he will have a prominent lower jaw • may have broad shoulders • even if slim may appear broad or plump • may be plump or tend to put on weight very easily

Behaviour and personality traits

The typical Cancerian man • is extremely sensitive • wears clothes with a conservative cut • does not like to be conspicuous • has some favourite old casual clothes which he always wears; he would be very cranky if anyone threw out his precious old jumper • does not push himself into the limelight • enjoys the limelight if it turns on him for a while • dislikes discussing his personal life • loves security, money, food and children • uses round-about tactics to get what he wants • has an uncanny business sense • is usually very attached to his mother

THE CANCER FEMALE

Appearance

The typical Cancer woman ● has a face that is typically round and soft but may be a crab-type as described above ● may be flat-chested or have a large bust ● has hips that are often slimmer than her bust ● puts on weight easily in middle age ● has a strong bone structure ● has very expressive eyes ● has long arms and legs compared with body ● has large and long or small and chubby hands and feet

Behaviour and personality traits

The typical Cancer woman ● is introspective and emotional ● uses her intuition more often than logic ● will use all her maternal instincts to care for and protect friends and family ● wants material security and comfort ● never does anything impulsively ● is shy but very sexual ● easily takes umbrage at minor insults ● is patient, subtle and often unconsciously manipulative

YOUNG CANCER

If a child behaves in a way that is distinctive of the personality associated with the zodiac sign of Cancer, he or she will have a tendency towards the characteristics listed below.

Behaviour and personality traits

The typical Cancer child ● changes mood frequently ● loves delicious food and drinks but almost always dribbles even when past babyhood ● is fascinated by colours and pictures ● will remember every experience right into adulthood ● longs to be hugged, loved, and encouraged ● withdraws inwardly from any kind of rejection ● can play alone for hours ● often invents invisible playmates ● may cry a lot and use tears to get what he or she wants ● when older, Cancerian children seek any kind of job to earn money and save it

CANCER AT HOME

If a person has the personality that is typical of those born with a Cancer sun sign, home is a place which must offer complete security and he or she will have a tendency towards the characteristics listed below.

Typical behaviour and abilities

At home, a Cancerian man or woman ● is capable of most kinds of DIY ● can cook and will keep a well-stocked larder ● feels safe and secure and so can relax ● will tend the garden ● may have collections of antiques ● spoils all visitors ● will hoard anything seen as potentially valuable

CANCER AT WORK

At work, the person who has a typical Cancerian personality will exhibit the following characteristics.

Typical behaviour and abilities

A typical Cancerian at work ● is there to make money ● takes work seriously and works hard ● will take responsibility ● responds to affectionate appreciation ● works steadily and is reliable

Cancer as employer

A typical Cancerian boss (male or female) ● expects his or her people to be neatly dressed ● takes work seriously and does not like frivolity ● has one aim: to make money ● drives a hard bargain but is fair ● rarely forgets anything ● generously rewards hard work

Cancer as employee

A typical Cancerian employee (male or female) ● will work hard for money because a good bank balance makes him or her feel secure ● will accept discipline calmly ● expects the rate of pay to increase steadily in response to increased output and responsibility ● enjoys taking responsibility

Typical occupations

Occupations that attract typical Cancerians are the food industry, such as baking, confectionery, catering, nutrition, hotel or domestic work; animal breeding, horticulture, gardening; anything connected with boats, water, ponds, rivers, fountains, baths, fishing; any kind of trading; counselling, psychotherapy, social services, nursing, obstetrics; political work connected with any of these.

CANCER AND LOVE

For a Cancerian, love thrives when there is a combination of constant affection with a healthy bank balance and substantial assets. A Cancerian in love will have many of the characteristics listed below.

Behaviour when in love

The typical Cancerian ● will rarely make the first move ● fears he or she will be rejected ● will retreat, deeply hurt, at the first sign of ridicule or criticism ● will respond to honest warmth and affection ● can become tenaciously attached to the loved one ● is a romantic at heart ● will put the loved one first in all things

Expectations

The typical Cancerian expects ● to be loved for ever ● to have his or her cooking appreciated ● to work hard for money and security ● the family to

come first in all things ● to be needed as a tower of strength and refuge
● unshakable loyalty and devotion

The end of an affair

The confusion between emotional hunger and love can lead to relationship
problems. Cancerians often feel they are not loved enough, and so make
draining demands on any partner who seems to have become disinterested.
The Cancerian will cling more tightly as a relationship deteriorates, making
separation very difficult. If the partner has been unfaithful, the Cancerian will
become very jealous and may react aggressively because the hurt is so great.
On the other hand, a Cancerian who feels unloved may secretly wander off to
find someone else to satisfy their strong emotional needs. Even so, they will
resist divorce, no matter how unpleasant the marriage becomes as a
consequence.

CANCER AND SEX

Love and sex are synonymous to the typical Cancer, as are love and marriage.
The Cancerian does not want a complicated sex life. The place where a
Cancerian makes love must be secure and help him or her to relax.
Cancerians tend to dramatize love and can become very strongly attached to
someone who never intended to make a commitment and therefore cannot
reciprocate their feelings.

CANCER AND PARTNER

The person who contemplates becoming the marriage or business partner of
a typical Cancerian must realize that Cancer will want to be the dominant
partner and will expect total devotion. Given this, the person who partners
Cancer can expect consideration, prosperity and a strong sense of belonging to
family or company. The contented Cancerian will never let the partner down.

Cancerian man as partner

He will want a partner who will mother him and take care of all the domestic
details, making sure he has a comfortable nest to return to after a day's work.
In marriage or business, he will want others around him. If the marriage proves
to be childless, adoption or fostering are likely. A business is itself seen as a
family. He will not usually enjoy working freelance.

Cancerian woman as partner

She will seek a partner as soon as she leaves the parental home – someone
who will luxuriate in her protective caring. She will devote herself completely to
the partner, even taking subtle control of him or her. A Cancerian woman will
want a family, and if denied the joy of children will acquire a household full of

animals instead. In business, she will be an excellent manager. The Cancerian wife is never a sleeping-partner when it comes to earning money. She will take a job outside the home to enhance the family's financial security.

CANCER AND FRIENDS

In general, Cancer likes friends who will support his or her emotional and financial needs when necessary – and Cancer will reciprocate.

Positive factors

Friends are, in many ways, regarded as family possessions themselves and are treated as such, with loving care, protective hospitality, sensitive consideration and great tenderness. Although some friends may come and go, friends from younger days are the most precious.

Negative factors

When he or she is hurt by a friend, the Cancerian anger may last for a long time and the friend may be abandoned. However, if the friend is an old friend, then the emotional attachment will finally lead to reconciliation. Cancerians do tend to set their own standards by the progress his or her friends are making. A compatibility chart, opposite, lists those with whom a Cancerian is likely to have the most satisfactory relationships.

CANCERIAN LEISURE INTERESTS

Not fond of heavy exercise, Cancerians may join clubs or causes that allow an outlet for making complaints and putting their maternal instincts to good use. Consumer affairs rouse their interest and they will follow popular interests in the arts. On the whole, typical Cancerians pursue the following leisure interests:
- boating, sailing, swimming ● water sports that are played in teams
- fishing and gardening ● keeping and breeding animals ● building collections
- keeping in contact with family members

COMPATIBILITY CHART

In general, if people are typical of their zodiac sign, relationships between Cancer and other signs (including the complementary opposite sign, Capricorn) are as shown below

	Harmonious	Difficult	Turbulent
Cancer	●		
Leo	●		
Virgo	●		
Libra		●	
Scorpio	●		
Sagittarius			●
Capricorn		●	
Aquarius			●
Pisces	●		
Aries		●	
Taurus	●		
Gemini	●		

CANCER LIKES AND DISLIKES

Likes

● anyone who loves his or her mother ● sentimental and family keepsakes
● gourmet food ● shopping trips ● history, especially family genealogy
● any demonstration of affection such as flowers ● a birthday card on the right date ● the company of other people ● a calm working atmosphere
● physical contact

Dislikes

● any tiny criticism of the home ● having to handle a crisis ● pressure to take part in conversation ● anyone who refuses their cooking ● people who forget names and dates (Cancerians have excellent memories themselves)

Leo: the Lion

23 July – 22 August

The fifth sign of the zodiac is concerned with ● pleasures, fun, playfulness, entertainment ● creativity, recognition, compliments ● romance, love affairs, sex, offspring ● children, child-like activities, childishness ● taking risks, gambling, sports, games ● performance, drama, limelight, applause ● entertainment, hospitality, appreciation

Elemental quality

Leo is the fixed fire sign of the zodiac. It can be likened to a fire burning in its proper place, such as a camp fire, a home fire in a grate or the fire at the centre of a medieval hall around which everyone can gather. Fire changes substances and Leos like transforming things with their energy. Being a fixed sign, Leos may be loyal, stubborn and proud of their achievements.

Spiritual goal

To learn the true meaning of love.

THE LEONINE PERSONALITY

These are the general personality traits found in people who are typical of this sun sign. Unhappy or frustrated Leos may display some of the not-so-attractive traits.

Secret Leo

Inside anyone who has strong Leo influences is a person who wants to be on top. Potential competitors should remember this. Leo is not interested in winning, but in being king or queen of a particular castle. Privately, the typical Leo craves love more than anyone would ever guess. Love, adoration, appreciation, recognition: these are what keep Leo's generous, fun-loving nature burning brightly. While typical Leos may appear to be confident, especially when they take centre-stage in the limelight, they have secret doubts about their true worth and may seriously undervalue themselves.

CHARACTERISTICS	
Positive	**Negative**
• Honesty and loyalty	• Stubborness or wilfulness
• A sunny disposition	• Contempt or arrogance
• A sense of dignity	• Sulkiness
• Pride in the home	• Smugness or boastfulness
• Attractive liveliness	• Indifference or an uncaring attitude
• Friendliness and kindness	• A tendency to take undue credit
• Generosity and hospitality	• A tendency to cut others down to size
• Acceptance of people at face value	• A tendency to keep up appearances
• A mature sense of responsibility	• Cold-heartedness when hurt
• Courageousness to the point of self-sacrifice	

THE LEONINE LOOK

People who exhibit the physical characteristics distinctive of the sign of Leo look majestic. They may seem tall if (typically) they are proud of their appearance. They are either very particular about their looks or apparently somewhat careless. Either way their appearance catches the attention of others – a usual Leo trait.

Physical appearance

• Body: slim and graceful in movement • Hair: long or short, bushy and curly or straight – a feature of pride which they emphasize by stroking, running their fingers through their locks or playing with a curl • Baldness: a Leo will either wear a fine hairpiece or make the bald head a feature! • Face: oval with large eyes • Voice: strong

THE LEO MALE

Appearance

The typical Leo man • has a well-proportioned body • is slim and athletic if he takes care of himself • if disabled will fight to regain prowess in some aspect of sport • has sex appeal and may be a playboy when young • walks tall with a noble bearing • dresses to impress

Behaviour and personality traits

The typical Leo man • likes to show off • is trusting • appears to be in control of himself • gives and expects loyalty • likes everything he does to be exciting • is generous with affection and money • likes an elegant environment • is popular • needs to be adored • uses charm to get what he wants

THE LEO FEMALE

Appearance

The typical Leo woman ● is slim and elegant ● if disabled will use this to advantage, making it attractive ● has sex appeal ● appears to possess an inner sense of royalty ● is well-dressed ● looks attractive even in adverse circumstances ● exudes dignity and class

Behaviour and personality traits

The typical Leo woman ● likes to show off in subtle ways ● is trusting and loyal ● is never docile or adoring in affairs of the heart but gives respect, warmth and real emotional commitment ● likes everything she does to be exciting ● is generous with affection and hospitality ● likes an elegant environment ● is a social leader ● needs to be admired ● uses courtesy to get what she wants

YOUNG LEO

If a child behaves in a way that is distinctive of the personality associated with the zodiac sign of Leo, he or she will have a tendency towards the characteristics listed below.

Behaviour and personality traits

The typical Leo child ● is sunny and friendly ● has a bottomless well of energy ● is more often on the move than still ● loves games and physical play ● when tired often falls fast asleep for a while ● loves to be the centre of attention ● adventurous and sometimes reckless ● likes to be waited on ● dislikes menial tasks ● loves parties ● is generous with whatever is seen as his or hers

LEO AT HOME

If a person has the personality that is typical of those born with a Leo sun sign, home is their natural territory and he or she will have a tendency towards the characteristics listed below.

Typical behaviour and abilities

At home, a Leo man or woman ● rules the roost ● creates an elegant, comfortable home ● offers superb hospitality ● expects others to respect his or her territory ● is able to fix most practical things ● enjoys entertaining ● shows courage and strength in emergencies

LEO AT WORK

At work, the person who has a typical Leo personality will exhibit the following characteristics.

Typical behaviour and abilities

A typical Leo at work ● gives a good first impression at interviews ● is able to act a part or exaggerate when necessary ● must be in charge of something ● can work very hard ● finds it difficult to apologize

Leo as employer

A typical Leo boss (male or female) ● has huge self-confidence ● can get everyone working hard for him or her ● loses confidence if his authority is undermined ● is thoughtful towards workers and their families ● is generous with praise and compliments ● enjoys showing people how to do things ● tends to take the credit for everyone's success ● cannot tolerate failure ● can charm people into working devotedly

Leo as employee

A typical Leo employee (male or female) ● needs to have his or her superiority recognized ● works hard ● is very loyal ● can keep customers happy ● makes a good showperson ● responds to genuine praise of his or her efforts

Typical occupations

Leo is often associated with leadership, promotion and sales, any job which has a special title, acting, directing, teaching, politics, public relations, management, the law or a self-employed trade. Leo often shows his or her inner strengths when under great pressure or when a crisis occurs.

LEO AND LOVE

To Leo, love is a dramatic ideal. Male Leos seem to have no trouble attracting women, while female Leos attract many men with their natural beauty and liveliness. The typical Leo in love will have many of the characteristics listed below.

Behaviour when in love

The typical Leo ● is romantic and proud of it ● becomes more regal and noble ● is very generous to the person who is loved ● is attentive and loyal to the loved one ● is radiant with happiness ● is caring, protective and supportive ● will make great sacrifices for love ● will fight to the death for the loved one

Expectations

The typical Leo expects ● to be adored by the loved one ● to be the envy of others ● to be treated like royalty ● his or her love to be seen as very special ● total commitment from the loved one ● the partner to be dependent in some way

The end of an affair

If Leo's passions cool, the partner is still needed, but more as a friend than a lover, which may cause problems and lead to parting or divorce if the partner does not like this arrangement. When a Leo wants to end an affair of the heart, pride may make it very difficult for the Leo to say straight out that things are at an end. Consequently, some Leos deal with this problem by withdrawing from contact or even by behaving badly towards the partner. If the partner does not confront the Leo and continues to cling, he or she can become quite psychologically cruel, treating the discarded partner with disdain. The partner who is unfaithful to Leo, or who walks out on a serious love affair, will leave behind a very wounded person. It will take Leo months to recover from such a deep hurt and may make him or her very wary of risking serious love again.

LEO AND SEX

When a typical Leo makes love it is regarded as a many-splendored thing. In fact, Leos can often forget about their partners as they wander through their personal, playful world of lovemaking. Leos are unrestrained lovers and can make the partner feel very special. Any idea of failure is alien to both male and female Leos. If sexual problems arise, a typical Leo is mortified and often will not seek the help that is needed. The sexual partner is also required to be a friend. In fact, the Leo wants love, sex and friendship from his or her spouse or lover.

LEO AND PARTNER

The person who contemplates becoming the marriage or business partner of a typical Leo must realize that Leo will believe him- or herself to be superior in some way or other. Given this, the person who partners a Leo can expect warmth, loyalty, support, generosity and undying devotion. Only lazy, foolish Leos look for a partner who will worship them.

Leo man as partner

He will want a partner who enhances his own image and who enjoys being in the spotlight as much as he does. The partner must be good-looking but should not outshine Leo himself. Leo man wants a marriage partner who will place him at the head of the table and believe in his dreams. She will be a woman of good manners who will never do anything to tarnish her own, and therefore his, reputation and she will be a devoted mother to their children.

Leo woman as partner

The typical Leo woman looks for a partner who will install her as queen of the whole neighbourhood. He must provide her with a house she can make into a welcoming place, where she can entertain with enthusiasm and be Lady Bountiful. With the right partner, a lady Leo will rise in social status due to her boundless strength and persistence. Consequently, her light will shine on her partner too. Leo woman will take the responsibility of motherhood in her stride and will expect her partner to be as devoted to the children as she is.

LEO AND FRIENDS

In general, Leos like their friends to be successful, but not so successful as to completely outshine and detract from Leo!

Positive factors

Leos are friendly, warm and often playful. They enjoy their friends and are proud of them; they are generous to their friends, but the friends are expected to show their gratitude, either in kind or by performance, putting Leo's support to good use.

Negative factors

A friend who in some way fails a Leo, perhaps by seeming to criticize or failing to appreciate something Leo sees as very important, may be dropped without explanation. A friend, partner or business associate who has personal aspirations may find it increasingly impossible to take second billing to a Leo, and so may end the relationship. A compatibility chart, overleaf, illustrates those with whom Leo is likely to have the most satisfactory relationships.

LEONINE LEISURE INTERESTS

Most typical Leos like to follow a fitness routine. Done sensibly, this will strengthen any weak points. As Leos always want to be outstanding in anything they do, they should beware of overdoing exercise – it may make them vulnerable to stress reactions. On the whole, typical Leos pursue the following leisure interests: ● any sport that offers skill with grace ● tennis, diving, running, dancing ● car driving, rallying, cycling ● theatre and dramatic activities ● family party games ● eating out

COMPATIBILITY CHART

In general, if people are typical of their zodiac sign, relationships between
Leo and other signs (including the complementary opposite sign, Aquarius)
are as shown below

	Harmonious	Difficult	Turbulent
Leo	●		
Virgo	●		
Libra	●		
Scorpio		●	
Sagittarius	●		
Capricorn			●
Aquarius		●	
Pisces			●
Aries	●		
Taurus		●	
Gemini	●		
Cancer	●		

LEONINE LIKES AND DISLIKES

Likes

● activity ● anything that promises pleasure ● being creative, e.g. gourmet
cooking ● receiving birthday cards ● beautifully wrapped, personalized
gifts ● silks, satins, gold ● receiving thanks ● an appreciative audience
● sincere compliments ● children and pets ● unusual food and new
recipes ● exotic drinks ● luxury furnishings ● top-quality, fashionable
clothes

Dislikes

● physical hurt ● sedentary activities ● being ignored ● being backstage
● lies and deceit ● being laughed at ● being told something they don't
know ● one-upmanship

Virgo: the virgin

23 August – 22 September

The sixth sign of the zodiac is concerned with ● self-perfection, critical faculties ● altruism, honesty, responsibility ● cleanliness, hygiene, health, healing ● efficiency, daily routines, reliability ● strength of character, veiled sensuality ● service, hard work, passivity, modesty ● incisive communication, shrewd logical thought

Elemental quality

Virgo is the mutable earth sign of the zodiac, indicating adaptable practicality. It can be likened to a semi-shaded patio which has been adapted to make a garden filled with a great variety of pot plants, climbers and an arbour. Half hidden, here and there, are garden loungers with rich patchwork covers, bottles of homemade organic wines and other unexpected practical delights.

Spiritual goal

To learn to discriminate between destructive criticism and simple wisdom.

THE VIRGOAN PERSONALITY

These are the general personality traits found in people who are typical of Virgo. An unhappy or frustrated Virgo may display some of the not-so-attractive traits.

Secret Virgo

Inside anyone who has strong Virgo influences is a person who worries too much about every personal imperfection and is never satisfied with his or her own standards. Virgo may appear to know it all and be a compulsive worker; both these behaviours hide a deep fear that he or she cannot be good enough for, say, the job or the partner. Virgos crave the opportunity to serve others and take charge of the many apparently mundane matters that, collectively, are the bedrock of success. One of the least suspected aspects of a Virgo personality is a strong, almost volcanic sexuality that can lie hidden and dormant for years until the right partner comes along.

CHARACTERISTICS	
Positive	**Negative**
• Gentleness with the helpless	• Scathing criticism of the lazy
• Sympathetic	• Cranky and irritable
• Humane and helpful	• Dogmatic
• Organized	• Untidy
• Knowledgeable about good health	• Tendency to be a hypochondriac
• Witty and charming	• Nervous and worried
• Physically sensual	• Prudish
• Painstaking	• Eccentric
• Emotionally warm	• Undemonstrative
• Dedicated	• Overdemanding

THE VIRGOAN LOOK

People who exhibit the physical characteristics distinctive of the sign of Virgo look neat and fastidious and have a pleasant, often quietly beautiful face. Many Virgos look like loners and are not usually noisy people.

Physical appearance
● High forehead ● Cranium may seem too big in comparison with the face
● Eyelids are often veiled ● Nose is straight ● Jaw is broad

THE VIRGO MALE

Appearance
The typical Virgo man ● has a straight, wedge-shaped nose ● has an extremely large forehead ● has a high hairline ● is upright and has a straight body ● may be quite tall ● often has one foot turned in more than the other

Behaviour and personality traits
The typical Virgo man ● is practical and unsentimental ● instinctively has a love of work ● will be devoted to serving those less fortunate than himself ● may relax by working a little less hard than usual ● takes responsibilities seriously ● is subtle and rarely obvious about his intentions ● notices and remembers details

THE VIRGO FEMALE

Appearance
The typical Virgo woman ● has a pointed chin and a face in repose ● the eyes are often soft and very beautiful ● the hair may be long or short but is normally impeccably groomed ● the mouth and lips are well formed ● is typically clean and very neatly dressed

Behaviour and personality traits
The typical Virgo woman ● can analyse situations in detail ● is devoted to her work, usually serving others ● is basically shy ● has incredible strength of purpose ● will pursue happiness wherever it leads ● is pure-minded but not naive ● thinks of herself as more orderly and efficient than other people ● has a delightful, straightforward personality ● does not express her feelings easily ● can be soothing one moment and critical the next

YOUNG VIRGO

If a child behaves in a way that is distinctive of the personality associated with the zodiac sign of Virgo, he or she will have a tendency towards the characteristics listed below.

Behaviour and personality traits
The typical Virgo child ● is quick, alert and an excellent mimic, and so can learn many things in a short time ● gets upset if he or she forgets something that has been learned by heart ● rarely questions authority but frequently questions facts ● is honest and reliable ● is usually shy among strangers ● loves to do jobs around the home imitating an adult ● is sometimes a fussy eater ● is usually tidy, with occasional bouts of disorganization ● gets very upset if teased ● is often an early talker and reader

VIRGO AT HOME

If a person has the personality that is typical of those born with a Virgo sun sign, home is a place where they will thrive, and he or she will have a tendency towards the characteristics listed below.

Typical behaviour and abilities
When at home, a Virgo man or woman ● enjoys being head of the household ● is domesticated in most areas such as cooking, managing the household finances, general maintenance, health, hygiene and gardening ● will always be doing or making something ● is usually at his or her most relaxed ● pursues several hobbies at or from home

VIRGO AT WORK

At work, the person who has a typical Virgo personality will exhibit the following characteristics.

Typical behaviour and abilities

A typical Virgo at work ● is best in a supporting role ● is meticulous and self-disciplined ● offers others a sense of stability ● is very helpful to other people ● can enjoy complicated, routine work

Virgo as employer

A typical Virgo boss (male or female) ● is excellent as boss of a small company ● can see the details very clearly ● will call a spade a spade ● expects honesty in all matters ● is kind-hearted, honest and fair ● expects good grooming, good manners and good habits ● can handle extremely complicated projects ● will reward good work with pay not perks

Virgo as employee

A typical Virgo employee (male or female) ● is good in service work or research, rather than manufacturing ● will become an excellent assistant to the boss ● does good work and expects correct pay ● is courteous, reliable and thorough ● is quick-thinking, analytical and intelligent ● will be cautious, critical and methodical

Typical occupations

Any occupation which enables the Virgoan to give service and handle complicated or difficult details will suit most Virgoans.

VIRGO AND LOVE

To Virgo, love is not dramatic, emotional or sentimental. A Virgo's love is devotion and will include love of family, friends and those less fortunate than he or she. Virgo in love with another person will have many of the characteristics listed below.

Behaviour when in love

The typical Virgo ● looks for quality ● is frightened by overt romance ● may wait for years for the right person ● once in love, loves warmly and steadily ● is devoted to the loved one ● will rarely give cause for any jealousy ● will do anything to avoid breaking up

Expectations

The typical Virgo expects ● devotion from the partner ● a sense of decency ● to enjoy platonic flirtation ● to be fussed over when feeling down ● personal matters to be kept private ● feelings to be handled with great care

The end of an affair

Virgos are typically loyal and will avoid ending a marriage or other permanent relationship whenever possible. However, in the long run, Virgos are sensible, practical people. If the Virgoan sense of fair play has been outraged, the Virgo will make a quick and final break, legally and in every other way. It is rare for a typical Virgo to linger in a fading marriage. If sensible, intelligent discussion does not solve the problems, the Virgo soon makes up his or her mind to end it. Reconciliation is not typical of Virgoan behaviour. Pleading, tears, sentimentality or a more aggressive approach will have no effect. Because the Virgoan has good self-discipline, the past is soon put aside. However, if children are involved, the Virgo divorcé or divorcée will want to ensure the children are properly educated.

VIRGO AND SEX

When a typical Virgo makes love it is a pure-minded, natural, healthy act. Virgo only enjoys sex when it is with someone who has gained Virgo's confidence. Celibacy, for short or long periods, is not usually difficult for a Virgo. In general, Virgoans are looking for a spouse, not a one-night-stand or an affair. A Virgo who has not had his or her fragile sense of self undermined in youth will enjoy sex. The bedside library may include informative books on sex, because Virgos like to understand the finer details. Virgo (male or female) tends to seduce with finesse, charm and subtlety. The fact that typical Virgoan instincts are chaste does not mean that Virgos are virgins. The Virgin of astrology is a symbol of self-improvement and fertility.

VIRGO AND PARTNER

The person who contemplates becoming the marriage or business partner of a typical Virgo must realize that Virgo will regard the union as permanent, although the finer details can be flexible. Given this, the person who partners Virgo can expect absolute loyalty. Virgos make strong commitments because they combine duty with devotion. Virgo will approach a proposal with great caution and will analyse the pros and cons thoroughly before getting involved. This is an excellent approach to any long-term partnership but may sound rather cold and clinical.

Virgo man as partner

He will be thoughtful, considerate and honest. He will remember dates, anniversaries and agreements. He can be a wizard when it comes to the sensible balancing of the budget. He will love, honour and criticize, but will not expect to be obeyed, waited on or be dazzled by sexy make-up and clothes. However, he will want cleanliness and a lot of warmth and sincere respect.

Virgo woman as partner

She is shy but as tough as nails when the need arises. In business she will be cool, intelligent and fully committed. Slow to love, Virgo woman is not interested in anything less than true love. When it happens, she will love intensely. She will only break a partnership if there has been hypocrisy. She is the most practical romantic in the zodiac.

VIRGO AND FRIENDS

In general Virgo likes a friend who is tidy, clean and intelligent with a broad range of interests. They prefer people who are not given to big shows of emotion and are attracted to those who offer a sense of peace and serenity.

Positive factors

Virgos love any pageantry that gives them an outlet for their tightly controlled emotions. Hence they are delightful companions at these events. Virgos are discriminating and have a fine artistic taste and a wealth of information on many subjects. They are not coarse and do not waste money. Virgos are loyal to their friends and will be extremely kind, considerate and helpful.

Negative factors

Virgos are nervous worriers, and a friend who in some way feeds the worries will reduce Virgo to a nervous heap. Virgos can be cold and critical, so a friend who softens the barbed remarks with caring laughter will bring out the Virgo wit. Most Virgos find it almost impossible to admit they are occasionally wrong. A compatibility chart, opposite, lists those with whom Virgo is likely to have the most satisfactory relationships.

VIRGOAN LEISURE INTERESTS

Most Virgos enjoy intellectual and practical pursuits. While many will take regular exercise for the sake of their health, they are not natural sportsmen and women. On the whole, typical Virgos pursue the following leisure interests:
● theatre, concerts, plays, pageants ● books, magazines, dictionaries, encyclopaedias ● detailed crafts, especially weaving ● cults, alternative medicines, psychology ● gardening, health foods, flowers ● computers with all the paraphernalia

COMPATIBILITY CHART

In general, if people are typical of their zodiac sign, relationships between Virgo and other signs (including the complementary opposite sign, Pisces) are as shown below

	Harmonious	Difficult	Turbulent
Virgo	●		
Libra	●		
Scorpio	●		
Sagittarius		●	
Capricorn	●		
Aquarius			●
Pisces		●	
Aries			●
Taurus	●		
Gemini		●	
Cancer	●		
Leo	●		

VIRGOAN LIKES AND DISLIKES

Likes

● making lists ● a well-stocked medicine cupboard ● self-inprovement courses ● punctuality ● mimicking others ● grooming self, taking showers, lovely soaps ● attending to the finest details ● very small animals, even ants ● being of service to others ● sensible, tailored clothes ● muted, subtle colours and textures

Dislikes

● crowds and noise; brash people ● slang, vulgarity, slovenliness and dirt ● people who whine and complain a lot ● sitting still for a long time ● disrupted schedules ● lids left off boxes, tins or toothpaste ● being under an obligation ● people who move Virgo's personal things ● hypocrisy and deceit ● any admission of weakness or failure ● bright, bold, primary colours

Libra: the Scales

23 September – 22 October

The seventh sign of the zodiac is concerned with ● partnership, relationships ● ideas, opinions, politics, diplomacy ● music, harmony, balance, romance ● tact, argument, self-control ● good manners, personal appearance ● refinement, sophistication, good taste ● rational thought, ideas for social well-being

Elemental quality

Libra is the cardinal air sign of the zodiac. It can be likened to a finely tuned wind instrument, producing powerful, moving music in perfect harmony. Air is the breath of life, and cardinal air is a metaphor for ideas put into action. Libras are doers rather than thinkers, although they may spend a long period thinking about a situation before making a decision and acting upon it.

Spiritual goal

To learn the meaning of selfless love.

THE LIBRAN PERSONALITY

These are the general personality traits found in people who are typical of Libra. An unhappy or frustrated Libra may display some of the not-so-attractive traits.

Secret Libra

Inside anyone who has strong Libran influences is a person who is terrified of being alone. The fear is usually well controlled so the typical Libra always looks calm, collected and in charge of the situation. Good-natured and loving, Libras can also be petulant, and even objectionable, when asked to take orders. Similarly, they are extremely intelligent, yet sometimes gullible; they enjoy talking to people, yet can also be very attentive listeners. The Libra symbol (the scales) is a clue to understanding this apparent inconsistency in behaviour. In the attempt to gain an even balance, the scales first tip one way and then the other. This is how the typical Libra behaves – constantly trying to attain that perfect balance.

CHARACTERISTICS

Positive	Negative
• Cooperative	• Narcissistic
• Good companion	• Indolent or sulky
• Artistic	• Fearful
• Refined	• Indecisive
• Has clear opinions	• Manipulative
• Good negotiator	• Overbearing
• Very strong beliefs	• Flirtatious
• Loving and romantic	
• Sense of fair play	
• Sincere	
• Charming	
• Communicative	
• An excellent mediator	

THE LIBRAN LOOK

People who exhibit the physical characteristics distinctive of the sign of Libra are not easy to describe, since there is no typical Libran feature, except for the dimple. It is a Libran habit to spend time deciding what to wear each morning, and to change clothes during the day if the occasion demands it.

Physical appearance
• Features are generally well balanced • Face is pleasant, even when angry
• May be a dimple in the chin, cheeks or knees • Charming smile

THE LIBRA MALE

Appearance
The typical Libra man • is usually handsome, but is never ugly • has a fine bone structure and balanced features • has a clear and very charming voice • dresses with discrimination in subtle colours • is usually graceful and athletic • likes to check his appearance in mirrors or as he passes a shop window

Behaviour and personality traits
The typical Libra man • is very keen to make a visual impression that is appropriate to the task in hand, whether it be an international conference, a romantic assignation or a day on the beach • gives advice freely • is interested in the opposite sex, at all ages • is a master in the art of romance • is very trustworthy • can be fickle and change his mind often • is interested in the facts of a situation so that he can come to a balanced decision • enjoys

art and needs harmony ● can be lavish with money, spending it on things that will bring happiness ● has financial abilities

THE LIBRA FEMALE

Appearance

The typical Libra woman ● is usually slim but curvy ● has large eyes ● has delicately flared nostrils ● has a large, well-shaped mouth ● has even teeth, often a gap between the front two

Behaviour and personality traits

The typical Libra woman ● is very aware of her looks ● takes care of her body and appearance ● uses her natural attraction to get what she wants ● presents her opinions with diplomacy and tact ● is excellent at partnership and teamwork ● loves luxurious clothes and perfumes ● has excellent powers of analysis ● will create a beautiful home

YOUNG LIBRA

If a child behaves in a way that is distinctive of the personality associated with the zodiac sign of Libra, he or she will have a tendency towards the characteristics listed below.

Behaviour and personality traits

The typical Libra child ● is a really beautiful baby ● hates having to decide between two things ● does not like to be hurried ● is fond of sweets ● always seems to know more about things than seems likely for someone of that particular age ● is kind-hearted ● likes to be fair and to be treated fairly ● can wheedle almost anything out of adults ● will obey rules if they are seen to be fair ● is usually neat and clean ● teenage Libras are romantics; they love warm water, bubble baths and lazy days in the sunshine

LIBRA AT HOME

If a person has the personality that is typical of those born with a Libra sun sign, home is a place to retire to for rest and recuperation, ready for the next period of sustained activity. The Libra will have a tendency towards the characteristics listed below.

Typical behaviour and abilities

When at home, a Libra man or woman ● will spend time just lounging around listening to music or reading pleasant books ● will enjoy arguing about almost everything with all the family – just for the sake of it ● uses good taste to create a place of harmony ● will be a very gracious host, offering good food and wines while making interesting conversation ● will keep the place tidy and clean, unless he or she has become resentful due to unfair treatment.

LIBRA AT WORK

At work, the person who has a typical Libran personality will exhibit the following characteristics.

Typical behaviour and abilities

A typical Libra at work ● takes time to get things right ● is usually honest in business ● is more often than not in a partnership ● is a great promoter of ideas ● builds a good network of contacts

Libra as employer

A typical Libra boss (male or female) ● is unhurried but extremely restless ● takes note of everyone's opinion before making decisions ● often suggests unusual answers to problems ● is an expert at the rational analysis of situations ● believes his or her policy is the best ● has strong opinions about finance

Libra as employee

A typical Libra employee (male or female) ● belongs to a union ● expects and gives a fair deal ● never gossips, although he or she talks a lot ● mediates effectively in personality tiffs ● can be moody, but is not nasty ● needs periods of rest

Typical occupations

Libra is liable to be involved with any aspect of the law, politics or diplomacy. Their eye for design may lead them into areas such as fashion, art dealership, or graphics. They will also enjoy working in jobs that involve talking and presentation, such as promotional work. Many Libras are good at planning business ventures.

LIBRA AND LOVE

To Libra, love is all. He or she tends to fall in love with love itself, and is eager to share life with the partner. The Libran ideal is a life that is filled with the peaceful, rosy glow of romance. Libra in love will have many of the characteristics listed below.

Behaviour when in love

The typical Libra ● is emotionally dependent upon the partner ● is casual and easy-going ● enjoys romantic settings ● will ignore the partner's shortcomings in return for love ● does not want a partner who is overly demonstrative ● glows with love for the whole world ● will do anything to avoid hurting the loved one ● gives the loved one complete attention

Expectations

The typical Libra expects ● to be supported and cared for ● faithfulness and loyalty ● to be free to get on with his or her work ● a partner to have his or her own separate interests ● to be amused ● to be admired and even exalted

The end of an affair

If a Libra is rejected, he or she is initially demoralized. However, the Libra quickly takes action to try to redress the balance that has been lost. Often the Libra will do everything to charm the loved one again, courting the partner as if for the first time. If the rejection is final, the hurt Libra will disguise the pain he or she feels by searching once more for true love. A Libra is most likely to reject a partner who makes too many demands on the Libran emotions. If this happens, the break will be as orderly and as well-mannered as possible.

LIBRA AND SEX

When a typical Libra makes love it is not always a passionate experience, unless there are more passionate signs in the Libra's chart. Libras may appear to be calm, confident and in control, but they are often very uncertain about their sexual identity. They are usually very influenced by images of sexual attractiveness in the media, and no matter how beautiful or handsome they are (and they often are) Libras can feel sexually very insecure and uncertain. All this does not, however, lessen Libra's interest in sex.

LIBRA AND PARTNER

The person who contemplates becoming the marriage or business partner of a typical Libra must realize that Libra forms partnerships to avoid the terrible sense of loneliness which is ever present at the heart of a Libra. Given this, the person who partners Libra can expect the marriage or the business to be happy and successful. Libra is the zodiac sign of partnerships, and typical Libras cannot imagine life without a relationship. The Libra will work hard and thoughtfully to make the partnership a harmonious balance of two personalities.

Libra man as partner

He will want a partner who has some good social or business connections. The young or immature Libra sees himself as the ugly duckling of the fairy tale. He will want his partner to be his personal mirror, reflecting back to him a self-image that is mature and confident. The developed Libra will indeed grow into a swan, but most Libras need plenty of encouragement on the way. In a partnership, Libra will generally take charge of the finances, making sure that there is always a good bank balance. Libras tend to have very strong views about money.

Libra woman as partner

The young, inexperienced Libran female will see a partner as the provider of all that she needs. As she matures, she will want to share herself with her partner. She will have plenty of talent and energy, and her aim is to be successful in every field. She will bring logic and sophistication to any business and a calm beauty to her home – where she will help her loved one to relax and to be renewed.

LIBRA AND FRIENDS

Libras are usually very social people who like to be on the go. Life for Libras revolves around keeping in touch with other people; this is what makes them happy. Libras will work hard for a friend, giving of themselves tirelessly for days on end. When they become tired, they will need to rest completely. But friends should not mistake the Libran recuperation periods as a loss of interest.

Positive factors

Libras are loving friends, and are unlikely to embarrass anyone with emotional outbursts. A Libran friend is honest and will treat a friend fairly. They make sensitive companions for visits to events concerned with the arts.

Negative factors

Libras can occasionally try the patience of a friend by their indecisiveness. They can be jealous of a friend who is better looking than he or she is. Friends must also be aware of the periodical depressive moods into which Libras seem to plunge. Such moods can be lightened by a genuine compliment. Friends should never forget that the worst thing for a Libra is to be left alone for too long. If this happens they can become irritable, sulky and very low in self-esteem. A compatibility chart, overleaf, lists those with whom Libra is likely to have the most satisfactory relationships.

LIBRAN LEISURE INTERESTS

Most typical Libras are not over-fond of vigorous, sweaty exercise. This offends their preference for a harmony of the senses. Whatever exercise they take, it must enable them to stay relatively neat and unruffled. Many Libras have a lasting interest in the arts. Of these, music is a high priority.On the whole, typical Libras pursue the following leisure interests: ● listening to music, studying music history, playing an instrument in a group, such as a string quartet or a jazz band, listening to poetry ● dancing, especially graceful styles ● dressing with sophistication ● eating out in romantic settings ● the scientific side of cooking ● computers ● any kind of discussion group

COMPATIBILITY CHART

In general, if people are typical of their zodiac sign, relationships between Libra and other signs (including the complementary opposite sign, Aries) are as shown below

	Harmonious	Difficult	Turbulent
Libra	●		
Scorpio	●		
Sagittarius	●		
Capricorn		●	
Aquarius	●		
Pisces			●
Aries		●	
Taurus			●
Gemini	●		
Cancer		●	
Leo	●		
Virgo	●		

LIBRAN LIKES AND DISLIKES

Likes

● pleasing surroundings ● getting notes, cards and flowers ● a good, detailed argument ● being fussed over ● being admired ● people running errands for them ● credit cards and store cards ● having people around ● attending to the finest details ● very small animals, even ants ● being of service to others ● sensible, tailored clothes ● muted, subtle colours and textures

Dislikes

● loud arguments ● confused situations ● sloppiness, especially in public ● ugly places ● being pressured to make up their mind ● being told it is up to them to make a change ● any criticism of their chosen partner or project

Scorpio: the Scorpion

23 October – 21 November

The eighth sign of the zodiac is concerned with ● birth, life, death, sex, sensuality ● passion, pushing boundaries of discovery ● regeneration, transformation, metamorphosis ● finance, investments, wills, inheritance ● hidden matters, secrets, taboos, magic ● collective unconscious, defence systems ● social revolution, reformation, change

Elemental quality

Scorpio is the fixed water sign of the zodiac. It can be likened to still waters that run deep. The relentless power of water to penetrate and transform even the hardest rocks is an excellent metaphor through which to understand the driving passion of the Scorpionic personality. Just as stalagtites and stalagmites cannot be prevented from growing, once started, Scorpio cannot easily be deflected from his or her purpose.

Spiritual goal

To learn the meaning of selfless love.

THE SCORPIONIC PERSONALITY

These are the general personality traits found in people who are typical of this sign. An unhappy or frustrated Scorpio may display some of the not-so-attractive traits.

Secret Scorpio

Inside anyone who has strong Scorpionic influences is a person who is intractable and impenetrable, so the secret Scorpio usually remains a secret. All Scorpios like to keep their true nature as hidden as possible. Astrologically, a Scorpio is said to be at one or other of three stages of evolution. A 'stage one' Scorpio exercises power through emotion and instinct. This Scorpio is symbolized by the scorpion, an insect more likely, in the end, to sting itself than others. The 'stage two' type exercises power through the intellect. This Scorpio is symbolized by the golden eagle – a bird that soars higher than any other. At the final stage of evolution, Scorpio exercises power through love. This Scorpio is symbolized by the dove of peace.

CHARACTERISTICS

Positive	Negative
• Self-critical	• Self-destructive
• Penetrating	• Ruthless
• Investigative	• Overbearing
• Passionately caring	• Suspicious
• Protective	• Jealous
• Tenacious	• Possessive
• Magnetic	• Dangerous
• Dynamic	• Quick-tempered
• Probing	• Obstinate
• Emotional	• Moody
• Sensual	• Sadistic
• Compassionate	• Insulting
• Concerned	• Secretive
• Unshockable	• Intolerant
• Intense	• Cunning
concentration	• Vindictive
• Understands failings	

THE SCORPIONIC LOOK

People who exhibit the physical characteristics distinctive of the sign of Scorpio have eyes that look at the world with almost hypnotic intensity. Eye colour and shape can vary widely, but if someone looks at you with deep penetration it is a sign of a personality strongly influenced by Scorpio.

Physical appearance

• broad face with wide forehead and thick neck • strongly built body of middle stature • generally slender with broad shoulders • intense eyes

THE SCORPIO MALE

Appearance

The typical Scorpio man • has strong features • has penetrating eyes • has thick eyebrows • has hairy arms and legs • has a well-proportioned figure • has an athletic body • has a tendency towards bow-legs

Behaviour and personality traits

The typical Scorpio man • is never self-effacing • is possessive of what he believes belongs to him • has to maintain his dignity • is a law unto himself and is most courageous in adversity • will give absolutely honest advice, appraisal or compliments • will move mountains to help someone • is intensely loyal to friends ● never forgets a kindness, or an injury ● can be a saint or a sinner, but pursues either course with great zeal

THE SCORPIO FEMALE

Appearance

The typical Scorpio woman ● has a compact and well-proportioned body ● has legs that are often short and thick ● is slender, but has a rather thick waist ● has attractive looks, even when frowning ● inclines her head downwards even when looking intensely at a person

Behaviour and personality traits

The typical Scorpio woman ● is poised and apparently cool ● never uses flattery ● only smiles when she means it ● wants total freedom of action ● regards flirting and flattery as insulting ● wants to dominate but can accept some restriction in order to win through in the end ● has many talents, all used with passion ● is loyal to family and home ● sets, and keeps to, her own standards

YOUNG SCORPIO

If a child behaves in a way that is distinctive of the personality associated with the zodiac sign of Scorpio, he or she will have a tendency towards the characteristics listed below.

Behaviour and personality traits

The typical Scorpio child ● enjoys a good fight and intends to win ● will learn only from a person seen as stronger ● keeps his or her own thoughts secret ● can find out everyone else's secrets easily ● has an instinctive understanding of adult problems ● can often bear pain well ● will be loving and loyal to family and friends ● will take revenge on others who break his/her favourite toys ● knows what he/she wants and goes out to get it ● is suspicious of strangers

SCORPIO AT HOME

If a person has the personality that is typical of those born with a Scorpio sun sign, home is a place to be proud of andhe or she will have a tendency towards the following characteristics.

Typical behaviour and abilities

When at home, a Scorpio man or woman ● makes the home self-contained ● is protective of children ● is gentle with the sick ● guards home territory jealously ● likes the home kept clean and orderly ● expresses good taste ● enjoys comfort

SCORPIO AT WORK

At work, the person who has a typical Scorpionic personality will exhibit the following characteristics.

Typical behaviour and abilities

A typical Scorpio at work ● will eventually know everyone's secrets ● will sense the moods of other people ● is indefatigable ● will excel as a team leader ● will appear to be calm in all situations

Scorpio as employer

A typical Scorpio boss (male or female) ● will demand total loyalty ● will do anything to help someone he/she likes ● will solve even the most difficult problems ● will never reveal the depth of his competitiveness ● confronts problems directly ● will be concerned and compassionate towards the workers' families, regarding them as part of the team

Scorpio as employee

A typical Scorpio employee (male or female) ● is self-motivated ● knows what he/she wants to achieve ● will take any amount of criticism from someone who has something he/she wants ● will accept failure as inevitable only when the odds are overwhelming ● is tenacious, intense and career-minded ● does not waste time and is not a clock-watcher

Typical occupations

Scorpios enjoy solving mysteries and penetrating the secrets of life. They love to get to the heart of any problem, human or mechanical. They may be detectives, pathologists, surgeons, scientists, researchers, undertakers, sewage workers, insurers, market analysts, butchers, members of the armed services or pharmacists. Any occupation which Scorpios feel is important and offers the opportunity to investigate and analyse complex problems will satisfy them. Scorpios can run a big business or a small enterprise as long as they feel that they are achieving something.

SCORPIO AND LOVE

To Scorpio, love is an intensely passionate and enduring emotion that may be directed at one person only. Love is central to the life of the typical Scorpio, and inspires many of their ambitions and actions. Scorpio in love will have many of the following characteristics.

Behaviour when in love

The typical Scorpio ● is deeply attached to the loved one ● attracts the loved one like a magnet ● is possessive ● hides emotions in public ● keeps dependence on the loved one hidden ● is faithful when in love ● dominates the loved one ● remains true to his/her own feelings

Expectations

The typical Scorpio expects ● absolute faithfulness and loyalty ● demonstrative love ● no great emphasis on romance ● genuine tenderness ● acknowledgement of how lucky the lved one is to be party to Scorpio's secrets

The end of an affair

If a Scorpio has an affair, it is often because the sexual life within the marriage has gone badly wrong. Scorpios seem able to attract partners without much effort, and will take the upper hand from the start, so that ending an affair is an easy matter. However, the Scorpio who is rejected is always very wounded and may want to take revenge. Some Scorpios immediately attempt to hurt their ex-partner. Others take their revenge in more subtle ways over a period of time. A rejected Scorpio is unlikely to forgive, and will never forget, the hurt.

SCORPIO AND SEX

When a typical Scorpio makes love it is an expression of all the pent-up passion that is hidden inside this most magnetic of personalities. Sex is an important element of life to a Scorpio. Indeed, Scorpio is the zodiac sign that indicates the greatest interest in sexual matters. As in other areas of their life, Scorpios are liable to be both inventive and single-minded – but for most Scorpios, sex is very much an expression of love.

SCORPIO AND PARTNER

The person who contemplates becoming the marriage or business partner of a typical Scorpio must realize that Scorpio will expect to dominate the partnership. Given this, the person who partners Scorpio can expect unwavering loyalty, hard work and a passionate drive to suceed – whether in business or marriage.

Scorpio man as partner

In business, the Scorpio man will inevitably be in charge of the partnership and is most likely to have initiated the terms of agreement. A Scorpio who accepts orders from a partner is doing so for a particular reason. For example, if money or future progress are the reward, Scorpio will appear to accept even a subordinate position for as long as it takes to achieve the results he wants. Scorpio will be proud of his partner and his partner's skills, and will go out of his way to enable the partner to achieve ambitions too.

Scorpio woman as partner

A Scorpio woman is often even more subtle than her male counterpart. She happily accepts the subordinate role and plays this part well. Again, however, this is only so that she can achieve her ambition in the end. Like her male counterpart, she will be loyal to the partner and do everything to help the partner. Scorpios can work very hard and they often provide the dynamism in a business. It is unlikely that Scorpio and her partner will have an equal footing. The Scorpio will, in reality, have the edge on the partner – but only in ways that the Scorpio sees will be helpful to the joint venture. Scorpio shrewdness is a vital asset in any partnership.

SCORPIO AND FRIENDS

In general, Scorpio likes a friend who recognizes Scorpio's magnetic superiority without fear or undue compliments. Scorpio chooses only a few friends and expects loyalty from them. Scorpio is not a natural socializer, but will keep close friends for many years.

Positive factors

Scorpios have good memories and enjoy telling jokes. They are generous and hospitable towards friends, and also make strangers welcome when they call for help or advice. Friends of Scorpios will be treated like family and given every help and consideration. Whenever Scorpio gives a friend advice it will be reliable. A friend can also trust Scorpio never to gossip.

Negative factors

Scorpios are unlikely to call on a friend without making an arrangement and having a good reason. Scorpios like others to do the calling. If they are out when a friend calls, their attitude is that it is the friend's loss, and that the friend will have to call again. Scorpios have an almost psychic insight into the motives and secrets of their friends. Anyone who dislikes someone knowing their secrets should stay away from Scorpios. A compatibility chart, opposite, lists those with whom Scorpio is likely to have the most satisfactory relationships.

SCORPIONIC LEISURE INTERESTS

Finding out how things work, taking something to pieces and reconstructing it, or delving into the mysteries of the human mind are all of interest to Scorpios, who also enjoy a variety of sports. Winning is important to them. On the whole, typical Scorpios pursue the following leisure interests: • any sport that demands shrewd tactics • competitive driving, flying or cycling • scientific hobbies • archaeology, anthropology, psychology • detective novels, treasure hunts, caving • breeding animals or plants

COMPATIBILITY CHART

In general, if people are typical of their zodiac sign, relationships between Scorpio and other signs (including the complementary opposite sign, Taurus) are as shown below

	Harmonious	Difficult	Turbulent
Scorpio	●		
Sagittarius	●		
Capricorn	●		
Aquarius		●	
Pisces	●		
Aries			●
Taurus		●	
Gemini			●
Cancer	●		
Leo		●	
Virgo	●		
Libra	●		

SCORPIONIC LIKES AND DISLIKES

Likes

● activity ● mysteries ● secrets ● winning ● sex ● being acknowledged
● home

Dislikes

● being analysed ● being asked personal questions ● people who know more than they do ● too many compliments ● having to trust a stranger

Sagittarius: the Archer

22 November – 21 December

The ninth sign of the zodiac is concerned with ● philosophy, idealism, religion, spiritual growth ● optimism, positive outlook, forward planning ● travel, freedom of movement, the outdoors ● generosity, honesty, justice, morality ● imagination, aspirations, open-mindedness ● wit, intellect, flashes of intuition ● generosity, pleasure, romance

Elemental quality

Sagittarius is the mutable fire sign of the zodiac. It can be likened to stars, a thousand lighted candles, the sparks rising from a rapidly spreading grass fire, or the reflectors marking the route along the centre of a major road. Fire changes substances and Sagittarians have a knack of transforming negative situations with their optimism. Mutable means adaptable. Sagittarians can adapt to almost any situation, whether earthly or spiritual.

Spiritual goal

To learn to use their talents to guide others.

THE SAGITTARIAN PERSONALITY

These are the general personality traits found in people who are typical of Sagittarius. An unhappy or frustrated Sagittarius may display some of the not-so-attractive traits.

Secret Sagittarius

Inside anyone who has strong Sagittarian influences is a person who wants to be free. Possessive partners, conservative thinkers, and bureaucrats that Sagittarius comes into contact with should be aware of this. No matter who or what the cause, the Sagittarian who is held back in life, in love or in opportunity for spiritual growth will be unhappy, even though he or she will keep smiling through all adversities. Like the centaur, one of the Sagittarian symbols, the Sagittarian personality experiences conflict between mind and body. The Sagittarian purpose is to overcome this conflict so that they may guide others.

THE SAGITTARIAN LOOK

People who exhibit the physical characteristics distinctive of the sign of Sagittarius look strong and active. They are often taller than average and have

CHARACTERISTICS

Positive	Negative
● Frank and open	● Argumentative
● Optimistic	● Impatient to be moving
● Sees the best in people	● Critical of those who deny their
● Honest and fair-minded	talents
● Spiritual	● A gambler at heart
● Enthusiastic	● Can be a fanatic
● Inspiring	● Hot-headed
● Disarmingly happy	● Fails to plan adequately
● Stimulating	● Tends to preach
● Happy-go-lucky	● Denies sadness
● Holds no grudges	● Uncommitted
● Sensual	● Fears any responsibility that
	curtails freedom
	● Blundering and inept
	● Indulgent

handsome faces. Since a typical Sagittarius is an optimist, the face often appears about to break into a smile – and regularly does.

Physical appearance
● Body: strongly built and energetic; movement is normally quick, although not always graceful ● Head: large, well-shaped skull with a high, broad forehead ● Uses hands and arms to make broad, sweeping gestures ● Bright, intelligent and sparkling eyes which often twinkle with good humour ● Either tall and athletic in appearance, or shorter with a sturdier body. Excess weight can be a problem, as Sagittarius is ruled by expansive, jovial, life-loving Jupiter

THE SAGITTARIUS MALE

Appearance
The typical Sagittarius man ● can be likened to a lively horse, and often has a mane of hair that falls over the forehead and has to be tossed away. In later life the Sagittarius may become bald, yet still retain a youthful look ● is physically noticeable, because of his strong sense of confidence ● will retain his physical faculties to a very old age

Behaviour and personality traits
The typical Sagittarius man ● is a risk-taker ● says exactly what is on his mind ● enjoys physical danger ● has an unerringly accurate wit ● has a good memory for facts, but often forgets where he has left everyday objects such as keys ● is trusting until let down ● can tell really funny jokes, but often fluffs the

punchline – which makes the joke even funnier ● may be tactless but is never deliberately cruel ● likes learning, study and creative interpretation

THE SAGITTARIUS FEMALE

Appearance

The typical Sagittarius woman ● has an oval face, a high forehead and a pointed chin ● has a tall and slender body ● has eyes that are steady, bright, open and honest ● has movement that is purposeful and even graceful

Behaviour and personality traits

The typical Sagittarius woman ● is honest ● enjoys freedom of thought and travel ● will laugh about her misfortunes and mistakes, even while she is upset or in pain ● is angry if her integrity is questioned ● is kind-hearted, though sometimes tactless ● can be deceived in romance, but is rarely misled in other areas of life ● enjoys taking risks, both physical and intellectual ● is often unconventional in relationships ● sticks by her own very clear moral standards ● can be cuttingly sarcastic when hurt ● regards herself and all others as equals

YOUNG SAGITTARIUS

If a child behaves in a way that is distinctive of the personality associated with the zodiac sign of Sagittarius, he or she will have a tendency towards the characteristics listed below.

Behaviour and personality traits

The typical Sagittarius child ● is a happy, playful little clown ● greets everyone and is despondent if others don't say 'Hello' ● acts on impulse ● is active, interested in many things and usually adores animals ● tends to get more bumps, bruises and cuts than many children because he or she is so adventurous, and rarely sits still ● gives and expects total honesty ● enjoys company ● when left on his or her own will hug a teddy or a blanket ● asks endless questions ● expects to be trusted

SAGITTARIUS AT HOME

If a person has the personality that is typical of those born with a Sagittarius sun sign, home is a place to rest the mind and body before moving off on the next trip. He or she will have a tendency towards the characteristics listed below.

Typical behaviour and abilities

When at home, a Sagittarius man or woman ● could be almost anywhere; Sagittarians make their home wherever they happen to be; some have, or would like, several homes, while others may be permanent travellers. It is not unusual for Sagittarians to spend time living abroad, or to divide their time between two different countries ● is usually planning for the next journey ● is not naturally domesticated ● enjoys making and receiving social calls ● does not enjoy formality, but loves informal gatherings where he/she is free to roam

SAGITTARIUS AT WORK

At work, the person who has a typical Sagittarian personality will exhibit the following characteristics.

Typical behaviour and abilities

A typical Sagittarian at work ● needs a challenge, so even in the dullest, most routine job, he or she will seek challenges ● is versatile ● needs to do several things at once ● may have two jobs ● needs intellectual and physical exercise ● gets tired only when bored

Sagittarius as employer

A typical Sagittarian boss (male or female) ● is rarely naturally tactful and may be quite blunt ● has a sense of overall planning, although they may overlook details ● expects people to be straightforward ● can be erratic and hard to tie down ● can promote anything extremely well ● can boost morale and will fight for what he/she believes is right ● is generally cheerful ● is kind and understanding

Sagittarius as employee

A typical Sagittarian employee (male or female) ● works best when allowed to get on with the job at their own speed – which is usually fast ● is cheerful and does not complain ● is enthusiastic, willing and generally ahead of everyone else ● enjoys praise and will promise almost anything ● is interested in current pay, but not in long-term career plans ● will boost everyone's spirits when they are downhearted

Typical occupations

Anything in sales and promotion that involves travel and knowledge of foreign languages; anything that allows Sagittarius to perform; and any career that involves learning and the use of the intellect such as teacher, barrister, or writer. A Sagittarius will be attracted to work that combines intellect and physical activity, such as veterinary practice, or indeed any kind of work with animals.

SAGITTARIUS AND LOVE

To Sagittarius, love is a romantic adventure. Sagittarius in love will have many of the characteristics listed below.

Behaviour when in love

The typical Sagittarius ● enjoys love on the move in foreign places ● is inventive ● needs good intellectual compatibility ● is totally honest with the loved one ● enjoys the physical pleasures of love ● is happy when he or she is loved ● is very generous and good humoured

Expectations

The typical Sagittarius expects ● not to be tied down ● to feel secure in love ● the loved one to be honest ● to retain freedom of movement ● to never be falsely accused of philandering ● to stimulate, amuse and be enjoyed by the loved one

The end of an affair

If a partner is possessive or jealous of Sagittarius, the relationship will begin to crack. Eventually, these pressures will cause Sagittarius to simply pack up and move on. Sagittarians enjoy meeting people and may indulge in the occasional affair. On the whole, the attraction of the affair wil be its excitement, rather than true romance. Sagittarius is prone to look elsewhere if an existing relationship becomes routine.

SAGITTARIUS AND SEX

A typical Sagittarius regards love as another adventure to be enjoyed and explored. Sagittarians tend to take a chance on love, and they enter a relationship with the same recklessness that they display in other activities. In the relationship he or she will be warm and loving, and a wonderful companion. Sagittarians normally enjoy a lot of touching and cuddling – a good, warm, loving hug is their form of security blanket. Common intellectual interests are equally essential to the success of any long-term sexual relationship.

SAGITTARIUS AND PARTNER

The person who contemplates becoming the marriage or business partner of a typical Sagittarius must realize that Sagittarius will value his or her freedom above everything. Given this, the person who partners Sagittarius can expect honesty and plenty of creative ideas.

Sagittarian man as partner

He will want a partner who enjoys spontaneity and who will appreciate his grand gestures and courageous outbursts of enthusiasm. He will also want a partner who will not try to control him. In business, a person who has a sound understanding of financial matters would make the perfect partner.

Sagittarian woman as partner

Frank and friendly, she wants a partner who can love her for her outspoken charm, not wilt under it. Her words and actions will always show what she is

SAGITTARIUS AND FRIENDS 71

thinking and feeling, so a potential partner should be quite clear about his own feelings. Sagittarian women are neither coy nor evasive, and will want a partner who does not play silly games. In marriage or in business, a partner must always ask her to do something, never tell her. However, she will respond to hints.

SAGITTARIUS AND FRIENDS

In general, Sagittarius likes a friend who is open-minded, ready for an adventure and trusting.

Positive factors

Sagittarians are friendly, gregarious people who accept any friend who matches up to their personal standards. They will defend a friend with great loyalty, but they will also say exactly what they think. Sagittarians have friends from many walks of life. Among those are likely to be both men and women, straight and gay people, a range of ages and a mixture of ethnic groups; they will all be treated as equals. Sagittarians respond to all calls for help. They will lend a friend money without expecting it to be repaid; they take in stray animals and stray people and will support any cause in the name of friendship.

Negative factors

Close friendship with just one or two people is not the Sagittarian norm. In fact, anyone who tries to get too familiar with, or who takes advantage of, the Sagittarian natural friendliness, may be struck by the fiery rocket of Sagittarian temper. They generally fight with words, as sharp as darts, but some may also use their fists. Sagittarians can be eccentric, and may find it difficult to keep a secret. A compatibility chart, overleaf, lists those with whom Sagittarius is likely to have the most satisfactory relationships.

SAGITTARIAN LEISURE INTERESTS

Sagittarians are versatile and like to kick against authority, so their leisure interests may be both varied and radical. Sports are natural activities for Sagittarians, who enjoy them for the social contact as much as for the competition. A Sagittarian who has not travelled is unusual. Long-distance travel to foreign places is one of the main Sagittarian interests. Some may prefer to 'travel' in the world of literature or religion, but their travels will also be far and wide. On the whole, typical Sagittarians pursue the following interests: ● gambling, gaming, racing cars, sky-diving and other risk-taking sports ● travel, exploration, cracking codes, tracking down mysteries, solving problems, speaking foreign languages, breeding animals, keeping pets ● religions, belief systems, new ways of being

COMPATIBILITY CHART

In general, if people are typical of their zodiac sign, relationships between Sagittarius and other signs (including the complementary opposite sign, Gemini) are as shown below

	Harmonious	Difficult	Turbulent
Sagittarius	●		
Capricorn	●		
Aquarius	●		
Pisces		●	
Aries	●		
Taurus			●
Gemini		●	
Cancer			●
Leo	●		
Virgo		●	
Libra	●		
Scorpio	●		

SAGITTARIAN LIKES AND DISLIKES

Likes

● freedom of action ● alternative ideas ● being on the move ● food and drink ● perfumes and beauty aids ● raffles and lotteries ● parties, flirting

Dislikes

● disapproval from others ● making promises ● being too safe, secure or confined ● administration ● tight clothes ● having their honesty doubted

Capricorn: the Seagoat

22 December – 19 January

The tenth sign of the zodiac is concerned with ● practicality, realism, hard work, accomplishment ● planning, determination, persistence, success ● high status, good quality, reputation ● responsibility, difficulties, problems ● paternalism, authority, discipline ● money, wealth, long-term projects ● wisdom, loyalty, sensitivity to beauty

Elemental quality

Capricorn is the cardinal earth sign of the zodiac. It can be likened to the oldest and most valuable tree in the forest. Sure-footed and thoroughly practical, in the end the Capricorn goat always reaches the heights, beating others who are faster but less determined. The cardinal signs must put their resources to good use. Earth resources represent practical skills: material, financial and social resources that can be used to further an ambition.

Spiritual goal

To learn to understand the feelings and needs of other people.

THE CAPRICORNEAN PERSONALITY

These are the general personality traits found in people who are typical of Capricorn. An unhappy or frustrated Capricorn may display some of the not-so-attractive traits.

Secret Capricorn

Inside anyone who has strong Capricornean influences is a person who worries about security – physical, social and emotional. A typical Capricorn cannot bear to be embarrassed in public. Sometimes, Capricorn longs to let go a little and to allow themselves to join in the fun – let their toes tap in time with the music. But usually a sense of duty and a terrible fear of looking foolish stop them from acting out their desires. Capricorns are also secret romantics who want a perfect and secure love in their lives.

THE CAPRICORNEAN LOOK

People who exhibit the physical characteristics distinctive of the sign of Capricorn generally have a small skeletal structure. The shape of the body will

CHARACTERISTICS

Positive	Negative
• Good organizing skills	• Tendency to believe their way is always the best
• Cautious and realistic	
• Hard working	• Egotistical
• Scrupulous	• A slave-driver
• Fearless	• Unforgiving
• Calculates risks but takes them when necessary	• Anxious, allows inner fears to dominate decisions
• Is an admiring spectator	• Takes a very critical view
• Has high but realistic standards	• A perfectionist who is never satisfied
• Conventional	
• Concerned	• Fatalistic
• Gives sound advice	• Status-seeking
• Loyal to tradition	
• Respects authority	

depend on how well the musculature has been developed. If physical training is part of Capricorn's routine, then it will be done with determination and discipline, resulting in a well-developed musculature which may make a Capricorn look heavier than he or she really is. A typical Capricorn has a serious look, and young Capricorns often look older than their years. It is also typical that ageing Capricorns eventually tend to become more relaxed and so look younger than their years.

Physical appearance
• Forehead: narrower than average between the temples, with deep frown lines
• Style of walking: swift and sure because all typical Capricorns take great care of where they put their feet when they take each step

THE CAPRICORN MALE

Appearance
The typical Capricorn man • is stockily built • has sharp, penetrating eyes • rarely smiles • has very strong white teeth • is conscious of his appearance • dislikes removing his clothes in public – for example, he will still be wearing a shirt during a heatwave when other men are bare-chested

Behaviour and personality traits
The typical Capricorn man • is dignified in his manner and very polite, regardless of his origins • seems unapproachable and self-protective • is totally reliable in pursuit of an aim • takes his time sizing up other people before he will relax enough to share his inner warmth • seeks honours but is

not interested in becoming famous; on the contrary, he avoids publicity ● has strong opinions but is not at all vain

THE CAPRICORN FEMALE

Appearance
The typical Capricorn woman ● small and well-shaped body with slender neck ● deep, serious eyes ● has an 'earthy' beauty ● full mouth and very white teeth ● shapely legs, slim ankles, small feet

Behaviour and personality traits
The typical Capricorn woman ● is very self-conscious ● behaves in a ladylike manner in public ● dresses according to what she intends to achieve that day ● needs to gain recognition for her work ● appears as steady as a rock, but is quite moody inside herself ● runs a well-kept home, although she finds domesticity tedious ● is totally loyal to close family and distant relatives ● cannot bear to be teased ● smiles little, but when she does it is a very beautiful smile

YOUNG CAPRICORN

If a child behaves in a way that is distinctive of the personality associated with the zodiac sign of Capricorn, he or she will have a tendency towards the characteristics listed overleaf.

Behaviour and personality traits
The typical Capricorn child ● tends to prefer older company ● often looks very old when still a baby ● is self-contained and strong-willed ● is usually even-tempered ● gets what he or she wants by slowly wearing down parental resistance ● likes the security of routine and orderliness ● has just one or two close friends ● enjoys pretending to be grown up ● usually loves reading ● likes to make things that have a practical use

CAPRICORN AT HOME

If a person has the personality that is typical of those born with a Capricorn sun sign, home is a place for enjoying the family as much as possible, and he or she will have a tendency towards the characteristics listed below.

Typical behaviour and abilities
When at home, a Capricorn man or woman ● really enjoys providing for the family and having visits from relatives ● likes having a routine and an organized household ● wants good quality furniture and fittings ● is basically loyal to home and family ● needs home as a safe haven for personal pleasure and business entertaining

CAPRICORN AT WORK

At work, the person who has a typical Capricorn personality will exhibit the following characteristics.

Typical behaviour and abilities

A typical Capricorn at work ● works hard and for long hours ● likes to have some home comforts in the workplace so he or she can change and go on to another appointment, or stay all night if necessary

Capricorn as employer

A typical Capricorn boss (male or female) ● does not neglect family life for business, and family members may visit him or her at work ● is kind but expects obedience to the rules ● has a strong sense of duty and works very hard ● is not a good mixer, but others trust him or her ● does not give perks but responds when people are in need ● takes responsibilities very seriously, and so may neglect personal needs ● dresses conservatively and is well organized ● can keep complex operations moving smoothly

Capricorn as employee

A typical Capricorn employee (male or female) ● arrives a little early and leaves late ● is dependable and can carry huge workloads ● minds his or her own business ● works steadily and quietly, staying with the same company a long time ● occasionally reveals a wry sense of humour ● is conscientious and aims high (for power not glory) ● will expect a salary in keeping with the work done ● has respect for superiors, elders and those more experienced ● enjoys commonsense procedures

Typical occupations

Any occupation that requires good organization and clever management, but which does not require the Capricorn to be the front person. Capricorns prefer to work in private. They generally make good bankers, systems analysts, bookkeepers, researchers, dentists, architects, engineers, manufacturers and politicians. Many Capricorns are jewellers, funeral directors, art dealers, anthropologists, and managers of musicians and other entertainers. They are also to be found on radio and television programmes; their quiet, unflappable natures are perfect for serious work under pressure.

CAPRICORN AND LOVE

To Capricorn, love is the source of all inspiration. Shy, awkward with the opposite sex and very much private people, Capricorns are, nevertheless, deeply interested in love and are reputed to be the most capable and loyal of lovers. Capricorn in love will have many of the characteristics listed below.

Behaviour when in love

The typical Capricorn ● is slow to make approaches and never flirts for fun
● only says 'I love you' when it is meant, and does not see any reason to keep
repeating it ● may worry about the emotional aspect of the relationship
● must feel financially secure to enjoy love ● is caring, considerate and
committed to the loved one

Expectations

The typical Capricorn expects ● to be taken seriously ● to make a long-term
commitment ● faithfulness ● privacy ● to make a home and family ● to be
admired by the loved one

The end of an affair

Typical Capricorns do not have casual affairs. If the relationship begins to fail, it
often takes Capricorns a long time to take action, as they have a strong sense
of duty to the partner and the family. In general, they dislike divorce. However,
once a Capricorn realizes he or she has made a mistake in choosing a mate,
then the parting will be abrupt and final. If a partner betrays a Capricorn, he or
she will try first to organize things so that the partner can be reunited with the
family, but if the betrayal continues, Capricorns can turn rather nasty.

CAPRICORN AND SEX

When a typical, mature Capricorn makes love, it is lovemaking at its very best:
to Capricorn there is no separation between love and sex. Capricorns know by
instinct when they have found the right partner for this immensely important
ritual. For some people sex is a release, the satisfying of one of the basic needs
in life, but Capricorns want to reach a state of total satisfaction, not only for
themselves but also for their partners.

CAPRICORN AND PARTNER

The person who contemplates becoming the marriage or business partner of a
typical Capricorn must realize that Capricorn will take over the organization of
the partner's working life. Given this, the person who partners Capricorn can
expect stability, security and success.

Capricorn man as partner

He will want a partner who can help him to achieve his ambitions. He will
want to organize the business, and will expect absolute loyalty and a
disciplined routine. He may assume that the partner is dependent on him.

Capricorn woman as partner

She seeks a partner who has a good, secure position in life already. She is more likely to make a bad choice of partner than the male Capricorn, but she will soon recognize her mistake. In business, Capricorn women do not often choose other women as partners. If the partner, in marriage or business, is lost through death or similar misfortune, Capricorns of both sexes find it hard to replace the partner, and will tend to withdraw into themselves.

CAPRICORN AND FRIENDS

In general, Capricorn likes a friend who is well bred, good mannered and not too extroverted.

Positive factors
Capricorns are loyal, kindly and often very generous to friends. They try to prove their sincerity by showing total devotion to the friendship, but this can go wrong if the choice of friend has been a bad one in the first place. They will continue to love a friend who is old or disabled. They will not desert or neglect a loyal friend, no matter how bad the circumstances.

Negative factors
Capricorns are not very good judges of character. If a friendship goes wrong, because of bad judgement in the first place, Capricorn may turn hateful. If a Capricorn suspects a friend of deception, he or she will start to suspect all friends. Sometimes Capricorn tests the trustworthiness of friends several times. Capricorns have an irritating habit of organizing things that they think will be good for a friend, which the friend does not want. At their very worst, Capricorns may use a friend to further an ambition without a word of thanks. A compatibility chart, opposite, lists those with whom Capricorn is likely to have the most satisfactory relationships.

CAPRICORNEAN LEISURE INTERESTS

Most typical Capricorns are not much interested in team sports. They will work hard at a hobby and want to make a success of it. Whatever they choose to do, it must be respectable and increase their chances of being admired or honoured. Capricorns are so aware of their duties and responsibilities that they often find it very difficult to allow themselves to enjoy anything for its own sake. As they get older and become grandparents, they tend to let loose a little and enjoy playing with their grandchildren. On the whole, typical Capricorns pursue the following leisure interests: ● music, listening or playing ● golf, walking, playing chess, tactical games ● visiting museums, galleries and the theatre ● reading, gardening, improving the home

COMPATIBILITY CHART

In general, if people are typical of their zodiac sign, relationships between Capricorn and other signs (including the complementary opposite sign, Cancer) are as shown below

	Harmonious	Difficult	Turbulent
Capricorn	●		
Aquarius	●		
Pisces	●		
Aries		●	
Taurus	●		
Gemini			●
Cancer		●	
Leo			●
Virgo	●		
Libra		●	
Scorpio	●		
Sagittarius	●		

CAPRICORNEAN LIKES AND DISLIKES

Likes

● hot, simple food ● antiques, history ● duties and responsibilities ● not being pressured by others, having plenty of time ● sexual love ● privacy ● what is regarded as the best, such as a Rolls Royce ● membership of an exclusive club ● home and family ● colourful food ● personalized gifts ● presents wrapped in magical paper ● new books ● diamonds

Dislikes

● untidiness ● being teased ● familiarity ● surprises ● new ideas ● loneliness ● being made to feel useless ● being embarrassed in public

Aquarius:
the Water Carrier
20 January – 18 February

The eleventh sign of the zodiac is concerned with ● scientific analysis, experimentation, detachment ● friendship, courtesy, kindness, tranquillity ● mystery, intrigues, magic, genius, originality ● eccentricity, independence, humanitarian issues ● fame, recognition, politics, creative arts ● electricity, magnetism, telecommunications

Elemental quality

Aquarius is the fixed air sign of the zodiac. It can be likened to a paraglider, jumping off the earth to explore a rainbow, yet aware of the practicalities of thermals and how to ensure a safe landing. Air represents the mind and the ability to think; Aquarian ideas may be unusual or even original, but once formed, they tend to remain fixed. Fixed air, in brief, is a metaphor for fixed opinions.

Spiritual goal

To learn how to develop true self-confidence.

THE AQUARIAN PERSONALITY

These are the general personality traits found in people who are typical of Aquarius. An unhappy or frustrated Aquarius may display some of the not-so-attractive traits.

Secret Aquarius

Inside anyone who has strong Aquarian influences is a person who is extremely uncertain of his or her true identity. The Aquarius ego is said to be the most precarious in the zodiac, probably because Aquarius is the sign of non-conformity. Intellectual genius, practical eccentricity and mental oddity are all linked with Aquarius. The typical Aquarius personality has a magnetic and powerful intellect. Putting this to good, practical use is the best way for Aquarius to build an identifiable ego.

CHARACTERISTICS	
Positive	**Negative**
• Communicative	• Unwilling to share ideas
• Thoughtful and caring	• Tactless and rude
• Cooperative and dependable	• Perverse and eccentric
• Scientific	individuality
• Strong belief in humane reforms	• Self-interested
• Independence of thought and	• Unwillingness to fight for beliefs
action	• Uncertainty and lack of
• Intense interest in people	confidence
• Loyal friendship	• Voyeuristic curiosity about
• Inventive	people

THE AQUARIAN LOOK

People who exhibit the physical characteristics distinctive of the sign of Aquarius often look like non-conformists.

Physical appearance

• There is a distant, dreamy look in the eyes • Body: taller than average • Head: in profile always noble with fine featuresnot usually noisy people. • Neck: bends to allow head to droop forward or tip to one side when thinking • Movement is not graceful but has purpose

THE AQUARIUS MALE

Appearance

The typical Aquarius man • is usually taller than average • has long bones • may have broad hips • is strongly built • has a distinctive facial profile • has a high, broad forehead

Behaviour and personality traits

The typical Aquarius man • is unwilling to reveal his feelings • is friendly towards everyone • is a group person • is fair-minded and has his own very strong, but personal, moral code • has wide interests • is attracted to the mysterious and the secret • is an intuitive thinker with a very practical streak • does not usually aim to become rich but to develop his ideas and communicate them

THE AQUARIUS FEMALE

Appearance

The typical Aquarius woman • may have broad shoulders • has a large bone structure • has a long neck • ignores feminine conventions, but always dresses in such a way that she looks stunning

Behaviour and personality traits

The typical Aquarius woman • has a wide circle of friends from all walks of life • is concerned about and deeply involved in the community • is adept at getting people to settle feuds • can be totally unpredictable • has a wide variety of interests and a mind of her own • will have a basic lack of self-confidence • can be easy-going and accepts the many differences among people

YOUNG AQUARIUS

If a child behaves in a way that is distinctive of the personality associated with the zodiac sign of Aquarius, he or she will have a tendency towards the characteristics listed below.

Behaviour and personality traits

The typical Aquarius child • is a quick thinker • is sensitive and intuitive • is outwardly calm, relaxed and delightful • is unpredictable and full of amazing ideas • wants to analyse everything and everyone • does not like emotional demands • rebels against commands and rules but comes to sensible conclusions when allowed to think things through for him- or herself • is generous to friends • has a huge number of friends of all kinds • tends to be absent-minded

AQUARIUS AT HOME

If a person has the personality that is typical of those born with an Aquarius sun sign, home is a place where he or she can fully express unconventional ideas. There are two types of Aquarius: the suave and the messy. He or she will have a tendency towards one of the sets of characteristics listed below.

Typical behaviour and abilities

When at home, a suave Aquarius man or woman • lives in a spacious, elegant apartment filled with interesting items • eats unusual menus of gourmet food • enjoys having houseguests from all walks of life When at home, a messy Aquarian man or woman: • lives in a tiny, untidy flat filled with oddities • eats strange mixtures of plain food • enjoys a wide variety of friends dropping in who feel at home in a creative mess • leaves inventions lying around • only washes up when in the right frame of mind

AQUARIUS AT WORK

At work, the person who has a typical Aquarian personality will exhibit the following characteristics.

Behaviour and abilities
A typical Aquarius at work ● enjoys working with a group ● usually likes to use his or her mind ● dislikes routine and decision-making ● enjoys variety

Aquarius as employer
A typical Aquarius boss (male or female) ● is fair and will pay employees exactly what the job deserves ● will be generous to anyone doing extra-special work beyond the terms of a contract ● although not a natural executive, he or she will carry out the role of boss using all the Aquarian skills of quick thinking and shrewd analysis ● will expect a day's work for a day's pay ● dislikes any form of dishonesty ● is unshockable ● will not forgive lies or broken promises ● will give employees all the rope they need (even to hang themselves)

Aquarius as employee
A typical Aquarius employee (male or female) ● is aloof but gathers a large circle of friends ● will regularly go off into a mental exploration of future possibilities – and return with some very creative ideas ● brings a fresh approach to any task ● will frequently change his or her job or type of occupation in the early years; later he or she will settle down and stay with one company ● is conscientious, courteous and has a knack for sensing what's wrong with machinery

Typical occupations
Anything that involves experimentation, ideas, investigation, analysis and forward thinking attracts Aquarius. For example: dancer, scientist, photographer, astrologer, singer, TV or radio presenter, writer, charity worker, inventor, archaeologist, radiographer, electronics engineer, humanitarian aid worker.

AQUARIUS AND LOVE
To Aquarius, love is an attitude of caring for all humanity. Aquarius in love will have many of the characteristics listed below.

Behaviour when in love
The typical Aquarius ● attracts the opposite sex in the first place by their friendly open manner ● may try to seem glamorously aloof ● is afraid of a deeply emotional involvement ● genuinely wants friendship with the loved one ● will guard his or her independence jealously ● enjoys a living-apart relationship

Expectations
The typical Aquarius expects ● his wife to stay at home ● her husband to share or take over the running of the home ● personal freedom of movement and action ● loyalty and faithfulness, which Aquarius will give in full once happily married ● understanding and tolerance of his or her oddities ● the partner to enjoy frequent visits from a wide variety of friends from every walk of life

The end of an affair

The typical Aquarius has only one love affair at a time and is devoted to that partner until curiosity leads them elsewhere. Aquarius, male or female, likes to dominate the relationship (as a way of controlling the feared emotions). A partner who makes too many demands, becomes jealous or tries to put limitations on Aquarius's freedom is usually dropped quite suddenly and may be treated like a total stranger. If the partner does not take the hint, Aquarius is quite capable of doing something to make the partner end the affair. Once Aquarius has settled into a marriage, he or she does not like divorce and will often want to remain friends with a past partner.

AQUARIUS AND SEX

When a typical Aquarius makes love it is more an intellectual experience than an emotional one. He or she will be most assiduous about hygiene and contraception. Aquarius is likely to do a lot of self-searching, but may not find it easy to listen to the partner's emotional problems. Aquarian partners often have verbal quarrels which seem to take the place of physical contact. Affairs do not seem to bother Aquarians, and they are rarely jealous. Many Aquarians make much better friends than lovers. Sometimes Aquarius can be rather modest about sex – even prudish.

AQUARIUS AND PARTNER

The person who contemplates becoming the marriage or business partner of a typical Aquarius must realize that Aquarius will need to have unlimited freedom. Aquarius will also want to dominate the partnership in order to ensure his or her interests in the wider world are not restricted. Given this, the person who partners Aquarius can expect loyalty, a fair share of the work and never to have the business taken away from them. Although Aquarius has no great driving ambition, the typical Aquarius has a very fine mind (one of the best in the zodiac) and can be an asset to any venture. If fame comes their way, the Aquarius partner will happily lap it up.

Aquarius man as partner

He will want a partner who recognizes the ideas and inventiveness that he can bring to the business, and who will allow him the freedom to introduce new concepts. Business partners contemplating asking an Aquarius to join them should first ensure that he has enough knowledge about the business. Aquarius man wants a marriage partner who will run the home and children and be a loyal, lifelong friend. He wants a woman who is capable of looking after herself, and who will not need to lean on him. A woman who wants a good income from a steady breadwinner should look elsewhere.

Aquarius woman as partner

So long as she is left to circulate freely among her many friends and pursue her dozens of outside interests, Aquarius woman will be a faithful partner. Although she can be tender and caring, she inhabits a world of ideas. She needs a partner who recognizes her brilliant mind. In business or marriage, Aquarius woman will be concerned that her partner is recognized for his intellectual achievements; she is far less interested in making money. She will enjoy physical closeness, but will also be happy with long periods when the relationship remains relatively platonic.

AQUARIUS AND FRIENDS

Aquarius makes many friends but has very few confidants. In general, Aquarius likes a friend who has intellectual interests and enjoys the unusual and the radical. Aquarius will be friendly towards anyone, and will tend to regard any relationship as platonic.

Positive factors

Aquarius rarely passes judgement upon the ethical codes of friends – but will expect them to live by their codes. Aquarius will put a lot of effort into his or her friendships and make friends with anyone: rich and poor, black and white, good and bad. An Aquarian friend is a constant source of mental stimulation, information and practical help.

Negative factors

An Aquarius will take a great interest in his or her friend's ideas, and may eventually adopt some of them as his or her own, using them whenever it is convenient. Aquarius tends to take over a friendship, slowly but surely, and put the friend under an obligation. Aquarius also pours out troubles to friends, expecting their concerns to be regarded as more important than anything else. However, when friends need help with their own problems, Aquarius tends to draw back and tell them to ignore the problem and it will go away. A compatibility chart, overleaf, lists those with whom Aquarius is likely to have the most satisfactory relationships.

AQUARIAN LEISURE INTERESTS

On the whole, a typical Aquarius will pursue the following leisure interests:
● radical arts and theatre ● music, rhythm, dance, controlled exercise
● clowning, juggling, witty comedy ● flying, parachuting, gliding ● writing his or her autobiography or a personal diary ● scientific or creative hobbies ● local politics

COMPATIBILITY CHART

In general, if people are typical of their zodiac sign, relationships between Aries and other signs (including the complementary opposite sign, Libra) are as shown below

	Harmonious	Difficult	Turbulent
Aquarius	●		
Pisces	●		
Aries	●		
Taurus		●	
Gemini	●		
Cancer			●
Leo		●	
Virgo			●
Libra	●		
Scorpio		●	
Sagittarius	●		
Capricorn	●		

AQUARIAN LIKES AND DISLIKES

Likes

● fame or recognition ● thinking about self privacy ● rainbows, dreams, magic ● change, eccentricity, surprises ● credit cards ● telling others what needs to be done – then watching them get on with it ● weird friends ● living within their means

Dislikes

● emotion and intimacy ● people who show off ● being taken for granted ● being pinned down in any way ● any kind of hardsell ● violence and fighting ● making loans or borrowing ● conventional authority ● revealing own motives ● extravagance

Pisces: the Fishes

19 February – 20 March

The twelfth sign of the zodiac is concerned with ● compassion, sympathy, love, altruism ● dreams, the psychic, precognition, sixth sense ● illusions, magic, film, fantasy, make-believe ● art, drama, music, poetry, prose, dance ● unusual talent, memory, wisdom, versatility ● sensitivity, intuition, humour, satire ● secrets, fulfilment of life, eternity

Elemental quality
Pisces is the mutable water sign of the zodiac. It can be likened to a warm, turquoise lagoon, twinkling in the sunshine, or to a strong ocean current rising from the depths to break over a rocky shore, smoothing the pebbles for all time. Mutable means changeable, and water can change its form in many ways: rain, hail, snow, mist, frost, clouds, rainbows, warm pools and puddles; thus Piscean feelings can change a dozen times a day.

Spiritual goal
To learn the meaning of peace through service to others.

THE PISCEAN PERSONALITY

These are the general personality traits found in people who are typical of Pisces. An unhappy or frustrated Pisces may display some of the not-so-attractive traits.

Secret Pisces
Anyone who has strong Piscean influences is a person who has perhaps the most extreme choices of any zodiac sign. Pisces can accept the challenges of life and rise to the top, or can give in to the easy way of oblivion and sink to the bottom. This choice is symbolized by the two fishes. To help him or her swim to the top, the Pisces must find peace through beauty, music and harmony. The Pisces needs work which will enable him or her to achieve this. More than any other sign, Pisces has many talents which may be used to develop their character. Many work hard to improve the lot of humanity. Others bring their talents to film and entertainment, enlivening the lives of thousands. Pisces needs to turn his/her private, mystical dream world of love and compassion into a reality. The only other option for Pisces is a life of illusion and, ultimately, a sense of failure.

CHARACTERISTICS

Positive	Negative
• Loving and caring	• Self-pitying
• Trusting, hospitable and will help all in distress	• Gullible and will give all in a lost cause
• Shy	• Temperamental
• Helpful	• Dependent
• Romantic	• Escapist
• Creative	• Sensationalist
• Mystical	• Depressive
• Gentle and kind	• Can lose touch with reality
• Compassionate	• Too emotionally involved with the problems of others
• Understanding of others	• Tends to blame self for everything

THE PISCEAN LOOK

People who exhibit some or all of the physical characteristics of Pisces look more clumsy than they actually are. They give off a feeling of other-worldliness, and usually have very sensitive, caring eyes. They may have a trusting, eager look or a quality of empathy and non-judgment exclusive to those who truly understand human sorrows and failings.

Physical appearance
• Body: usually short and thick-set • Back: may stoop as the person walks
• Eyes: a sleepy appearance with large eyebrows • Head: oddly shaped
• Limbs: generally short

THE PISCES MALE

Appearance
The typical Pisces man • may be tall but is not physically distinctive • has a somewhat clumsy appearance • has rather heavy jowls • has broad or thick shoulders

Behaviour and personality traits
The typical Piscean man • has few prejudices • is not ambitious for status, fame or fortune, although he can make good use of opportunities if they come his way • is very romantic • cannot easily be fooled • has few material needs, but needs his dreams • talks slowly and is knowledgeable on many subjects • is rarely jealous, but gets hurt all the same • is emotionally involved in whatever he does, although he may never show it

THE PISCES FEMALE

Appearance

The typical Pisces woman ● is normally slim, but tends to put on weight easily in later years ● has large eyes and an oval face ● has a clear, soft skin, whatever her colour ● has an air of feminine mystery ● has a very warm, charming smile

Behaviour and personality traits

The typical Pisces woman ● does not try to dominate her partner in any way ● often appears vague and dreamy ● is subtle and, while appearing to be helpless or incapable, gets things organized and manages the finances extremely well ● protects her emotional vulnerability with humour or a sophisticated exterior ● needs to belong to someone ● has a warm, sympathetic heart

YOUNG PISCES

If a child behaves in a way that is distinctive of the personality associated with the zodiac sign of Pisces, he or she will have a tendency towards the characteristics listed below.

Behaviour and personality traits

The typical Pisces child ● has the sweetest, dimpled smiles and the most winning ways of all babies ● lives in a world of make-believe ● dislikes orderliness and routines ● has an amazing imagination ● holds secret conversations with invisible (and sometimes long-dead) people ● has a very active sixth sense ● believes in magic, fairies and Santa Claus, and may re-invent myths ● enjoys the company of adults more than that of other children ● rarely loses his or her temper, and instead just happily goes his or her own way

PISCES AT HOME

For a typical Piscean, home is the place where he or she will need to feel loved. Home can be a palace or a hovel, but it must contain people towards whom he or she is drawn emotionally and who love him or her.

Typical behaviour and abilities

When at home, a Pisces man or woman ● will often enter a fantasy world ● will feel safe to freely explore his or her imagination ● will probably have no fixed routine ● is likely to be untidy, although he or she may have a sudden urge to tidy everything to avoid confusion: this can happen at any time ● should keep a large, clear clock ● will need a space for personal privacy ● will make the home itself into a wonderful world of art, music, design, and good food and wine

PISCES AT WORK

At work, the person who has a typical Pisces personality will exhibit the following characteristics.

Typical behaviour and abilities

A typical Pisces at work ● is rarely in an executive position, nor does he or she enjoy being in a team that has a strict routine ● enjoys work that offers freedom of expression, which usually means working alone or in a self-directed position ● if working in a team, Pisces prefers an occupation that allows for frequent changes and adaptations

Pisces as employer

A typical Pisces boss (male or female) ● is more likely to be found in organizations as a director rather than as the boss ● will serve people rather than accumulate power ● uses his or her gifts to make the correct move ● is a shrewd judge of character ● is unconventional and creative ● values those who are conventional and well organized, because they are needed to back up his or her ideas ● will never refuse help to someone in need ● may act tough to hide a deep belief in the mystical

Pisces as employee

A typical Pisces employee (male or female) ● needs work where there is plenty of outlet for either human understanding or creative imagination ● will be depressed, lazy and useless if neither of these needs are satisfied ● will be very affected by surroundings ● when happy is a loyal worker ● although nobody seems to understand how he or she operates, Pisces gets the job done

Typical occupations

All kinds of jobs in film, theatre, TV, radio, ballet, music and art will attract Pisces, who is often a good actor. A job that allows travel will be attractive. Advertising, public relations and any job that is part of the service industry. Helping people to solve their problems, charitable and church work are also very attractive to Pisces.

PISCES AND LOVE

To Pisces, there is no difference between love, affection and romance. A Pisces needs all three. A Pisces who feels unloved is an unhappy person to whom life seems very grey. Love revitalizes Pisces.

Behaviour when in love

The typical Pisces ● is romantic ● eager to please ● adapts to the demands of the relationship ● appears to be helpless, delicate and vulnerable, but being loved enables Pisces to cope very well with a range of difficulties, problems and tragedies ● is emotionally involved, to the point of not recognizing when he or she is being deceived or treated badly

Expectations

The typical Pisces expects ● to have his or her dreams valued, and to be protected from harsh criticism ● to be cared for romantically ● to have children (Pisces love children) ● to be frequently reassured that they are loved ● all birthdays and anniversaries to be remembered

The end of an affair

Some Pisces tend to drift into another relationship almost without noticing, yet are surprised when they are accused of unfaithfulness. The self-doubt which haunts many Pisces can only be dispelled by repeated reassurance that they are lovable. Consequently, Pisces may sometimes just leave a relationship for no clear reason and with no regrets. It is not that Pisces does not love the abandoned partner anymore. On the contrary, Pisces will often show much sympathetic understanding and will try to retain a friendly relationship with the one he or she has left. The worst possible event for a Pisces is to be rejected by the one who loved them. A partner who wants to end a relationship with a typical Pisces will find this a very difficult thing to do. Pisces will cling, convinced that if they reform in some way, everything will be all right again. The ex-partner of a Pisces may have to go to extremes to extricate him- or herself from the emotional mess that a hurt Pisces can produce.

PISCES AND SEX

When a typical Pisces makes love it is an act of romance rather than of carnal pleasure. Typical Pisces is less interested in sexual activity than in the expressions of love that come before and afterwards. Piscean energy is more often used up in the emotional experiences of love than in the sexual act. This does not mean Pisces is not interested, indeed he or she may seek several partners, but this is for reassurance rather than personal pleasure. Pisces can be the least prejudiced and most compassionate of all the zodiac signs. Pisces will show a deep and real love for a partner who has problems or physical abnormalities, or who has to face a tragedy or business disaster.

PISCES AND PARTNER

The person who contemplates becoming the marriage or business partner of a typical Pisces must realize that Pisces will expect to be supported – emotionally or financially. Given this, the person who partners Pisces can expect loyalty and sensitive understanding.

Pisces man as partner

He will want a partner who will work for him: someone to run the household efficiently and who will entertain his friends and business colleagues. In return, the married Pisces will bring great joy to a household with his wonderful imagination. Potential business partners should be prepared to undertake the practical, administrative side of the business, leaving the Piscean partner free to exercise their creativity and understanding.

Pisces woman as partner

She will want a marriage partner who will support her in every respect. To many men, Pisces is the perfectly feminine woman. She may appear to be a helpless, fluffy person but, once married, she will feel secure and her reserve of talents and abilities will pour out in every direction. In business, a Pisces woman will be best in creative positions and in public relations, but should not be expected to do the routine office jobs.

PISCES AND FRIENDS

In general, Pisces likes a friend who is useful and reassuring. In return they will give unprejudiced understanding and loyalty to their friends.

Positive factors

Pisces are emotionally attached to their friends and will rarely notice if the friend is taking advantage of this involvement. Pisces are friendly, humorous and caring friends, even if there are long periods of time between meetings. Pisces will always think up something interesting to do, and will enjoy any kind of artistic ventures.

Negative factors

Pisces can be a confusing person, so arrangements may be difficult to make. Pisces can sometimes seem to be cool and off-hand. This is usually temporary and due to a moment of insecurity. Pisces needs a hero or heroine to identify with. If a friend happens to be the chosen one, this can be pleasant enough but may become a nuisance when Pisces gives the friend talents he or she hasn't got and expects them to be demonstrated! Pisces does not find it easy to conform; friends with conservative attitudes may find this a difficulty. A compatibility chart, opposite, lists those with whom Pisces is likely to have the most satisfactory relationships.

PISCEAN LEISURE INTERESTS

Most typical Pisces love artistic pursuits and anything that has an element of mystery, fantasy and imagination. Pisceans love films, theatre, travelling entertainers, pantomimes, witches, monsters, elves, gypsies and mythical creatures. Team sport is not a natural Piscean activity, but Pisceans often love gentle watersports, non-competitive skiing and sky-diving. Dangerous sports, such as racing cars, can also appeal to the Pisces because they have an unerring instinct in such situations.

COMPATIBILITY CHART

In general, if people are typical of their zodiac sign, relationships between Pisces and other signs (including the complementary opposite sign, Virgo) are as shown below

	Harmonious	Difficult	Turbulent
Pisces	●		
Aries	●		
Taurus	●		
Gemini		●	
Cancer	●		
Leo			●
Virgo		●	
Libra			●
Scorpio	●		
Sagittarius		●	
Capricorn	●		
Aquarius	●		

PISCEAN LIKES AND DISLIKES

Likes

● seafood, champagne and organic foods ● romantic places, sunsets over the sea, mountain vistas, waterfalls, ponds and waterlilies ● background music, poetry ● people who need their understanding ● mystical settings, candles, incense ● being loved ● freedom to drift along from time to time ● privacy ● colourful food ● personalized gifts ● presents wrapped in magical paper ● new books ● diamonds

Dislikes

● bright, noisy, crowded places ● dirty, ugly objects ● being told to get a grip on things ● stiff clothing ● authorities ● people knowing too much about him or her